HOW TO SEE
BIRDS

HOW TO SEE

BIRDS

An Enthusiast's Guide

Matthew Stadlen

Foreword by Martin Harper
Global Conservation Director, RSPB

To David Howarth, my godfather and uncle, who helped inspire me to become a birdwatcher, and to my wife, Lily Walters, who has encouraged me in my birdwatching and photography and who now has a keen eye for a distant raptor.

— Matthew Stadlen

First published in Great Britain in 2019 by Papadakis Publisher

 **PAPADAKIS**

An imprint of Academy Editions Limited

Kimber Studio, Winterbourne, Berkshire, RG20 8AN, UK
info@papadakis.net | www.papadakis.net

 @papadakisbooks  PapadakisPublisher

Publishing Director: Alexandra Papadakis
Design Director: Aldo Sampieri
Publishing Assistant: Megan Prudden

ISBN 978 1 906506 69 8

front cover: Kingfisher, Rye Meads, Hertfordshire

back cover: Swee Waxbills, Kirstenbosch Botanical Gardens, Cape Town, South Africa

half title: Cuckoo, Thursley Common, Surrey

frontis: Lilac-breasted Roller, Masai Mara, Kenya

opposite: Orange-breasted Sunbird, Kirstenbosch Botanical Gardens, Cape Town, South Africa

CONTENTS

FOREWORD

MARTIN HARPER

GLOBAL CONSERVATION DIRECTOR, RSPB

There are some things we take for granted: the passing of the seasons, the rising and the setting of the sun and even the wildlife that we often ignore as we carry on with our hectic lives. But if we only took time to stop for a few moments and look up, we would be reminded of the majesty of the natural world, the beauty of bird song and the artistry of flight.

In this delightful book, Matthew shares his personal encounters with wild birds. Through his exceptional photographs and commentary, his passion and attention to detail shine. From the common to the rare, he treats each subject with equal reverence, and they are, rightly, the stars of the book.

I have two favourite photos.

The first is of a greylag goose preening. I have a soft spot for this relatively common species (which has been re-established by humans in many parts of the UK) as we have had a breeding pair nest on the pond in the gardens of the RSPB's Headquarters in Sandy, Bedfordshire. The drama of rearing a young family plays out in full view of RSPB staff and visitors to the Lodge.

The second is of the cuckoo – alert and intense. This iconic species not only provides the soundtrack to our summer but acts as a reminder that our nature is shared because it spends just 6-8 weeks in the UK. The rest of the year it is either migrating or on its over-wintering grounds in sub-Saharan Africa.

Yet, like many of our migratory birds, the cuckoo is in trouble – having declined by 65% since the mid-1980s.

In fact, there are 44 million fewer birds today than there were when England won the football World Cup in 1966 – with the majority of species in decline. We have not treated the other species with whom we share this planet with the respect that they deserve. We have destroyed or polluted their homes, persecuted them and made it harder for them to rear their young. To live genuinely in harmony with nature, our own species needs to change.

That starts with us opening our eyes to the world and wildlife around us. Matthew has shown how he has seen birds and I am sure that you will enjoy this splendid book. More than that, I hope that this book inspires you to get out, really look for birds and most importantly feel motivated to take action to protect them for now and for future generations.

Meadow Pipit, Pembrokeshire

INTRODUCTION

W hen you see a bird, do you *really* see it? I ask because it's perfectly possible to go through life with an almost total disregard for birds. Some people positively dislike them – something about their beaks perhaps, or their feathers? Most are simply indifferent. But many of us do show at least some interest in the avian world. There are, in Britain, more than a million members of the Royal Society for the Protection of Birds. And thanks to Instagram – and other networking sites – there is also a growing number of bird photographers opening our eyes to unimagined treasures.

In fact, the opportunity to share my own photographs easily and to learn from others has rekindled in me an interest in birds that waned during my twenties and early thirties. Social media has made photographers of us all and an occasional twitcher of me. I sometimes drive long distances just to see and photograph a species for the first time. Without the buzz of uploading the results, I would not have made the effort. In the process, I have rediscovered the thrill of birdwatching.

I'm not an expert – either in birds (although I'm beginning to hold my own with those who are) or photography. I don't know much about cameras. I've only recently worked out how to use the manual focus on my Nikon camera. But I do have a strong sense of what I think is beautiful and a passion for birds that has its roots in childhood. What I lack in expertise, I make up for in enthusiasm, and in this book I hope to show you that we can all become witnesses to – and even chroniclers of – the breathtaking beauty on our doorstep and beyond. If I can do it, so perhaps can you.

Wheatear, Pembrokeshire

Becoming a better photographer is as much about being disappointed in what hasn't worked as it is about celebrating what has. I've never been on a photography course in my life so, for me at least, it really is a case of trial and error. You learn just as much from that almost-amazing-shot as you do from the rare occasions when you produce an image of which you are proud. The essential thing is to take an interest in the bird. The more you understand about your subject, the better the photograph is likely to be. And it's a virtuous circle: the better your photography, the more you're likely to understand the birds – and appreciate their intricacies.

In the past four years, I have watched Honey Buzzards circle high above Italian fields, crept close to hummingbirds hovering in Santa Barbara and witnessed the Cuckoo, blue grey in the morning light, calling in the Oxfordshire countryside. There is a story behind every one of the birds with which I have chosen to illustrate this book, and I will tell you the tale of how I photographed each one.

As a national radio host on LBC, my schedule affords me the freedom to escape into the countryside between shows. But whether you live in an inner city or in the Welsh hills, the beauty of birds is within your reach. The moments I have treasured most are scattered far and wide, from my bedroom window in London – from where I've watched Goldfinches nesting on the wisteria – to the southernmost tip of Africa. Even as I write these words, I'm momentarily distracted by the sight of a Sparrowhawk circling above my terraced house.

A 2004 study found that nearly three million people aged over 15 go birdwatching in the UK regularly or occasionally but, when I was growing up, it wasn't 'cool' to be able to tell the difference between a Blue Tit and a Great Tit. Enthusiasm, though, is contagious, and as bird photography booms, more and more of us seem to be waking up to the lavish variety of bird life in our midst. My wife would once have raised an amused eyebrow had I pointed out a pair of Bullfinches making their way from branch to branch. Now, she has a beady eye of her own for distant raptors.

It always struck me as rather odd that taking pleasure in the natural world around us, whether we live in towns and cities or in a remote rural paradise, should be considered quirky or, worse, the object of ridicule. Yes, there are the life lists, the species counts, the hint of competition too, but at its core, birdwatching is – for me certainly – about immersing oneself in nature and sharing our planet with wildlife. Anyway, what's wrong with being a nerd?!

I was brought up in west London and still live a handful of tube stops from Oxford Circus. Birdwatching helps me to escape the thrust of a busy metropolitan life – even when I'm taking photographs metres from my

Nubian Woodpecker,
Masai Mara, Kenya

front door. The stresses and strains of the daily routine melt away as an elusive Coal Tit distracts the eye and disappears briefly into the bosom of a tree in blossom.

My fascination with birds really began, though, when a then Edinburgh-based uncle took me, aged eight, on a trip to the edges of the Highlands in search of Golden Eagles. We soon spied the giant bird of prey, high in the sky. Although its six foot wingspan was dwarfed by the distance, it was a landmark moment for me to witness arguably our most magnificent bird flying high above the mountains. We found a pair of young Ospreys, too, perched on their nest, just before they headed for warmer climes in Africa.

Birds of prey immediately impressed me. Which was the strongest? Which the quickest? Easily the Peregrine Falcon, it turned out, with its plunge for prey thought to be as fast as around 200 miles per hour! The Red Kite may have lost some of its mystery since its reintroduction has made it a familiar sight on the London to Oxford road, but I'll always remember years ago watching one soar above the valley in Powys where my parents have a country home. With its white head, red plumage and distinctive forked tail, it remains a favourite British bird of mine.

At first, in awe of the mighty eagle and the stubborn buzzard, I was troubled to learn that they were capable of being ganged up on by smaller, less spectacular species such as the Crow or Magpie. Mobbing, it's called. But soon I began to see the beauty in the tiny Goldcrest, the cock-tailed Wren and the shy Redwing.

Most importantly of all, however, I have come to realise that travel is not a prerequisite of a successful day's birding. You don't have to be in remote corners of the globe to enjoy birds, nor even in the Welsh countryside. Wherever you are in the British Isles, you are likely to be within eyesight, or at least earshot, of a surprisingly extensive range of species. I've counted more than twenty in my parents' garden alone. Not bad for central London! From the loping Grey Heron crossing the rooftops to the miniature Long-tailed Tit flitting through the bushes, from the Green Woodpecker to the graceful Mute Swans flying

in formation overhead, birds are at ease in our towns and cities. There really is beauty all around us, if only we lift up our eyes to see.

Not to forget pricking our ears to hear. For too long I was deaf to the myriad melodies of the avian chorus. No longer. Bird song is often an indispensable guide to identification, and it can be the sweetest of music, too. Listen out for the Blackcap singing in the spring and the common Blackbird with its bright yellow bill, warbling from the tip of a rose bush in summer. What better soundtrack to a morning with camera, or binoculars, in hand?

Birds aren't only aesthetically alluring either – they're incredible achievers too. Take the Willow Warbler. It is little more than 10cm long, but when it arrives on our shores in spring, this bundle of green, yellow and white will have flown five thousand miles to reach our lenses across desert, sea and mountain from Africa. Some long-haul flight!

Maybe it won't surprise you that many birds can navigate vast distances using rivers, roads and coastlines as signposts. It certainly amazes me that juvenile Cuckoos are able to migrate successfully despite never having met their parents. How they are programmed to find their way is one of the great unsolved mysteries of nature. They also represent a challenge to the photographer, too: adventurous as they are, they're also shy and difficult to capture.

There are, of course, birds that we never see on British shores, and I have packed my love of ornithology with me in my hand luggage as I've travelled around the world. Wherever you are, Peru, New Zealand, Spain or Pakistan (where I saw Black Kites scavenging above the dusty streets of Lahore), there can be a revelation around every bend in the road. During a stay near the Point Reyes Peninsula in Marin County, just across the Golden Gate Bridge from San Francisco, I added around 60 species to my tally (yes, I do have a list!). In all, I've seen something like nine hundred, although I've only been able to identify two thirds of them.

I'll never forget, while camping in the hills near Nelspruit in north eastern South Africa, happening upon the

Paradise Flycatcher in rather inauspicious surroundings. I was using the makeshift outdoor loo, shielded only by bushes, when a cocktail of colours with a long tail hovered above my head. The contrast between the grimness of my circumstances and the magnificence of the bird couldn't have been more pronounced.

Birdwatching certainly appeals to the collector in me. Racking up species gives me the sort of pleasure that I imagine trainspotters derive from adding the 12.26 from Doncaster to their lists. Part of the joy in encountering my first Barn Owl, pale brown and white against the winter snow of early 2013, was that I hadn't ever seen one before. But there are other, deeper needs, that watching birds fulfils.

Meditation is one. I've never found sitting still and urging my mind towards emptiness to be an easy experience. But sometimes, when I'm birdwatching, I lose myself as profoundly as more conventional meditators might lose themselves.

This is how it works: I take myself off to a sunlit wood early in the morning. At first I can't see a single bird; but then I spot one. A Marsh Tit perhaps. In following the trajectory of that tiny bird, I am led on to others and then others that sing and call in the boughs of the trees. Soon I have become almost part of their avian society, as close as I will ever get to nature – in body and mind. Almost all other thoughts and sense of self fade away for a few precious minutes.

Creativity, as I have begun to explain, is the other need that birdwatching now satisfies in me. When I first started posting photos on Instagram, I mixed oversaturated sunsets with comically filtered landscapes. Gradually, though, birds became the focal point. Today I don't even own a pair of binoculars and travel instead with my camera. It has a 500mm zoom and can reveal astonishing detail even at considerable distances. And if I'm unable to identify a bird with the naked eye, I can compare my photographs with the guide book in the car or the phone in my pocket.

Here's a memorable example: For decades, I'd wanted to see a Merlin. It is Britain's smallest bird of prey and something about the contrast between its neat features

and deadly will intrigued me. While I was out looking for Hen Harriers in the Cambridgeshire Fens, a flock of birds sprung into the air in a terrible frenzy, startled from the bushes. Almost immediately, two peeled away from the crowd and darted to the left. Within a moment I realized that this was a chase and that, in fact, one of the pair was a miniature raptor, not much larger in size than its prey.

Kestrels have been known to attack clustered birds on the wing but this hunter seemed too small and the behaviour more characteristic of a Merlin. To my huge frustration, though, because I wasn't quick enough with my camera, I couldn't be certain. Only months later, when I managed to capture with my lens a darting grey shape flying close to the ground on the Oxfordshire wetlands, was I sure that I had, finally – and at the age of 37 – seen a Merlin. The image might have been blurred, but the bird's identity wasn't in doubt. Such excitement!

There's a social side to bird photography, too. I was able to match a face to an Instagram account when I got chatting to a hospital doctor on the wetlands of Otmoor, an RSPB reserve in Oxfordshire. And when one of my listeners on *LBC* began following me on the same app, I discovered her brilliant bird photos and she gave me directions to find the Little Owl she had snapped in a London park.

There are those who take birdwatching several steps further. Twitchers are people who, on learning that a rare species has arrived in another area, travel sometimes hundreds of miles to see it for themselves. While I was still working at the BBC, I discovered via a colleague's Twitter account that two Bearded Tits were feeding among the bulrushes by the Diana Memorial Fountain in Hyde Park. The male is one of our prettiest birds, with a russet cloak, azure head and the black beard that gives the species its name. I wanted to see one of these unusually beautiful and comically named birds for first time, so I went, with my mother, to the park and found them by the water.

More recently, I have driven far further in pursuit of rare visitors. Perhaps most excitingly, after a long trek to the Essex coast, I saw my first Rough-legged

Buzzard. But I am an amateur by comparison to Lee Evans, a famous twitcher I once spotted on a Norfolk beach while I was among a group of birdwatchers attempting to distinguish between an Isabelline and Desert Wheatear. Lee reportedly travelled around 70,000 miles in a single year to see 352 of the 390 species that were recorded in the UK in 1992.

However you choose to enjoy birds, if you buy yourself a pair of binoculars or a half decent camera, you won't be treading a lonely path. There's a thriving community of birdwatchers up and down the country, and it's easy to make friends along the way. And, as became obvious to me when when I presented a BBC documentary at Bempton Cliffs in East Yorkshire about the RSPB, there are also teams of committed bird-lovers who dedicate considerable energy and effort to the conservation of our landscapes for the benefit of our feathered friends. It is important to remember, too, that whether we are out to take photographs or just to look, the welfare of the birds we're looking for should always take priority.

Meanwhile, we are a step closer to joining the ranks of countries that can boast a national bird. America has the Bald Eagle, Norway the White-throated Dipper and Greece the Little Owl. Now we Brits, unofficially at least, have the Robin. The chirpy red-breast saw off competition from the Barn Owl and the Blackbird to win ornithologist David Lindo's poll of more than 200,000 people in 2015. The Robin, which, unlike most birds, can seem happy in human company as it hops in the footsteps of gardeners, is described by Lindo as being "as entwined into our national psyche" as a "Christmas card pin-up".

Just as playing and watching sport adds to my life, so too does watching and taking photographs of birds. Capturing a Rufous-breasted Hummingbird sucking pollen out of a Californian flower or tracing the flight of a Peregrine across the Welsh hills with my lens couldn't be much more different to watching England take on Wales in rugby. But it's no less exciting. And whether the millions of British birdwatchers and I are cool or not, a love of ornithology is something I'll carry with me forever.

To help understand how birds behave, I have divided the species in this book into groups: 'Garden Birds'; 'Countryside Birds'; 'Water Birds'; 'Visitors'; 'Foreign Birds'; 'Owls' and 'Birds of Prey'. These categories sometimes overlap and I've had to make judgement calls as to which grouping best suits some of the birds I describe. So, for example, I have placed all the raptors in the same chapter, whether or not I spotted them in Britain or abroad, and I've located Sedge Warblers in the countryside category even though they might just as well have joined Cuckoos and Nightingales in the section about visiting species. The birds that illustrate the garden section could almost all have found a home in the chapter about the countryside, but I wanted to emphasise how birdwatching is a hobby that we can do in our own backyard even if we are urban dwellers.

This book is neither guide nor gospel. Rather, I intend it to be used as the key to a magical world that remains unexplored by so many of us here and abroad. If you already have an interest in birds or wildlife photography, I hope what follows serves to deepen your passion for the natural world. Starting with the smallest bird in each chapter and building towards the biggest, I want to take you, with the help of my photographs, on a very personal birdwatching journey and, in the process, encourage you to see birds – to *really* see birds! From the giants of our skies to the sweetest singing Garden Warbler, from my London street to the Indian jungle and taking in countries as far afield as Albania and Australia, this is, in a way, also a story of my life.

Jackdaw, Richmond Park, London

Garden Birds

One of the surprising joys of birdwatching is that, even if you live in the heart of a big city, you don't have to stray far to experience a variety of bird life. Where I live in Notting Hill, I've listened to Goldfinches nesting in the wisteria that runs up the front of our house. They are painted in the colours of the German flag – red, gold and black (with some white thrown in too) – and it's a privilege to share our home with such a spectacularly pretty bird. Like foxes, they seem to be thriving in an urban environment and they can enrich our daily lives.

Although it was the scale and power of birds of prey that first drew me into the avian world, it didn't take long before I began to appreciate birds of every shape and size. The tiny Goldcrest, no bigger than the noisy Wren and similar in colouring to its rarer cousin the Firecrest, drew my attention upwards to the forest canopy on the fringes of our family garden in Mid Wales and more recently caught my eye as I sat in the dining room of a house in Sussex. Long-tailed Tits danced in busy throngs along the paths of the communal garden where my brothers and I played football as boys. My parents live in the same house they lived in when I was born, and only the other week, my mother spotted this eponymous bird, pretty in pink, white and black, among her rose bushes. It was good to learn that the species remains a local resident.

We may have done much to diminish our environment but, ironically, as farming continues to eat into natural habitats, birds seem to be flocking ever closer to us, finding refuge in towns and cities, and treating us to their comings and goings in our backyards.

Country gardens are visited by Nuthatches, Flycatchers – Spotted and Pied – and fished in by Kingfishers and Grey Herons. Wherever we live, there is an obvious abundance of wildlife on our doorstep. A Magpie, glossy in black and blue, recently hopped along the wall just metres from my window. If you look, if you *really* look, you'll find beauty in the commonest of our birds and you don't have to get in the car or travel on public transport to find the treasures in our midst.

Goldfinch,
Otmoor, Oxfordshire

COAL TIT (11.5cm)

Coal Tits are common. But – and there should be no need for a 'but' – the intricacies of their patterning and delicate shifts in their colouring demand our attention. Immediately distinguishable from their scarcer relatives the Marsh Tit and (rarer) **Willow Tit (11.5cm)** by the white nape that splits the black of their neck – and lacking the funky hairstyle of the **Crested Tit (11.5cm)** – they are pretty little birds. Catch them at a bird feeder in an RSPB hide on the picturesque banks of Lake Vyrnwy in Powys and they'll dart nervously in and out of view. Not much bigger than a thickset thumb, they make their way between the heftier Chaffinches and more confident Siskins, determined to have their fill of the plentiful seeds.

Tiny acrobats among the branches, Coal Tits are perhaps most at home in conifer forests where they can be found hanging upside down to access food. But they're adaptable creatures too, happy to nip in and steal seeds and nuts from garden feeders before storing them safely out of the reach of bigger, more dominant birds. In winter they can team up with other tits to form flocks in pursuit of something to eat. Look out for that black and white head and the cinnamon fringe to the underparts.

opposite: Coal Tit, Notting Hill, London

below left: Crested Tit, St Moritz, Switzerland

You don't have to live near a Welsh lake to encounter a Coal Tit. In fact, you need not get up from your armchair, even if you are in the centre of a city, to join in the fun of birdwatching. Urban birding can be as rewarding as a stroll in the country. In my parents' London garden I've spotted Green and Great Spotted Woodpecker, Wood and Feral Pigeon, House Sparrow, Blackbird, Blackcap, Greenfinch, Goldfinch, Grey Heron, Mute Swan, Canada Goose, Long-tailed Tit, Great Tit, Blue Tit, Song Thrush, Mistle Thrush, Crow, Robin and no doubt others that I'm forgetting.

Just up the road from my childhood home, no more than a hundred yards from the Ladbroke Grove traffic, I recently spent a shimmering spring afternoon watching a Coal Tit singing at the peak of its voice amid the cherry blossom. As I photographed the bird, its tiny body entombed in pink and invisible to most pedestrians, a delivery man wanted to know what on earth I was up to. Urban birdwatchers are understandably objects of curiosity, and we struck up a conversation. Twenty minutes later, I knew more about Islam than I had before setting out with my camera, and I'd made a new friend, too. Following a passion is contagious, often sparking the interest of others, and we can be at our most approachable when we're lost in what we love.

below right: Willow Tit, St Moritz, Switzerland

BLUE TIT (12cm)

At their most quintessentially colourful, Blue Tits are a mix of bright blue and yellow with a smattering of green. Though not quite so tiny as Coal Tits, they are indeed distant relatives of the giant eagles that roam the higher skies. Common visitors to bird feeders up and down the country, Blue Tits are among our least shy garden companions. But it would be a shame to overlook their smart, striking tunics just because their faces are so familiar. I photographed three tits hanging out on a pole in our neighbour's front yard down the lane from my parents' home in Wales. As you can see from the photograph, they were not so brightly coloured as some, but they make a pretty picture. I became transfixed in my attempts to capture the little birds as they darted to and fro from the food that had been put out for them.

Bolder in colour and noticeably bigger, too, than the Blue Tit is the **Great Tit** (**14cm**), which, although a woodland species, has also made a home for itself in towns and cities. Before I knew better, I mistook its repetitive two note song for the Chiffchaff and I would listen to it in the early hours of the morning from my London bed. I photographed a fine example of the species in Richmond Park and its yellow tummy is offset by the pale greens of the background. Look out for its distinctive black head which immediately sets it apart from the Blue Tit.

below: Great Tit, Richmond Park, London

opposite: Blue Tits, Powys, Mid Wales

GOLDFINCH (12cm)

British birds tend not to be as spectacular in their plumage as many of their more exotic counterparts. Visit Cape Town, as I did recently, and you may be wowed by the Orange-breasted Sunbird; travel to Australia and you could encounter the Sulphur-crested Cockatoos that I watched feed on a coastal balcony in Victoria when I was 19. But there are dramatically dressed species here, too, and the Goldfinch is imperious in red, yellow and black. The birds that nest in our wisteria offer intimate sightings and I've been lying in bed while a resident, oblivious of me, has been perched within centimetres of the windowpane.

Spring is a time of furious activity for these noisy, chatty birds as they dive to and fro between our home and the big plane tree that looms above the rooftops opposite, and I have photographed one from my front door on a sunny afternoon. They can, though, be tricky to capture in their multicoloured elegance. Shoot from front on, and you'll miss the golden streaks of the wings. On one of my trips to the Otmoor reserve in Oxfordshire in search of rarer species, I managed to capture the bird in all its glory. With its back to me but its head tilted sideways, the Goldfinch revealed a whole golden stripe together with its blood-red face. Sitting on the stump of a tree with a mottled green backdrop, it's almost as if this often restless bird was posing just for me.

Keep a lookout for Goldfinches in your garden, whether in town or country. Their pronounced and sharp-looking beaks enable them to dig out seeds from thistles and teasels. They often breed in 'loose' colonies, according to the RSPB, and I've seen them in small flocks bouncing along a lane or over a field in jerky flight. Their gold feathers prominent, they are a whir of colour and call.

I have happy memories of searching the urban gardens of a sun-soaked Santa Barbara for avian life in March, 2016. Cedar Waxwings crowded a tree that neighboured the house we were staying in, hawks flew overhead and hummingbirds hovered like tiny helicopters at the mouths of exotic flowers. I think I even glimpsed – though I can't be sure – a Golden Oriole skulking in a tree and I certainly photographed a blurry American Goldfinch for the first time. Though smart in yellow and black, it lacks the red cheeks of its iconically coloured European relative.

Although our Goldfinch can be found in many parts of the world, and many British Goldfinches themselves migrate as far south as Spain in the winter, I associate it with the rural landscapes of England and Wales – and now, of course, with my home itself.

Goldfinch,
Otmoor, Oxfordshire

SISKIN (12cm)

A bird I wanted but failed to see as a boy but that turned up at my mum's feeders in Wales in my twenties or thirties. The male is a riot of yellows and greens with a prominent black crown; the female, also streaky in appearance, is duller and lacks the black on her head. I've now seen many of these petite finches, which are more common in Wales and Scotland than in England, and photographed several. The male I captured from an RSPB hide at Lake Vyrnwy has a ring on his leg which indicates that his movements are being tracked in a low tech way by someone with a licence to research bird behaviour. Look out for the forked tail and sharp beak that Siskins use to tear at seeds.

Siskins are not unlike Serins, although the latter are very rare in the UK and my sightings have been confined to France and maybe to Spain when I was on a trip through Andalucia with my father in my early teens. Only on my most recent holiday in the Luberon, where I've stayed with my family at the same dreamy villa almost every year for a decade, did I notice Serins singing energetically from the conifers and other outposts of the property. They were, however, too elusive to photograph up close, despite my best efforts in the heat, so I've made do with my pictures of Siskins here.

opposite: Siskin, Lake Vyrnwy, Mid Wales

below: Siskin, Powys, Mid Wales

ROBIN (14cm)

The Robin seems even more at home in our gardens than the Blackbird. Known as the gardener's friend for its habit of following in our footsteps in search of worms and bugs thrown up by the churned earth, there is a sweetness as well as a poignancy to the Robin Redbreast. According to legend, the bird comforted Jesus on the cross by singing into his ear and its breast was stained red from Christ's blood.

Robin, Notting Hill, London

There is certainly a traditional connection between Robins and Christmas. The birds that adorn festive cards are thought once to have been a symbol of the red-jacketed Victorian postmen, known as 'Robins', delivering the cards. Still, charming as they appear to be, don't mistake Robins for gentle souls within the bird world. Males are highly territorial and will attack intruders belonging to their own and other species.

I've photographed Robins far and wide, hoping to capture the famous bright breast, sometimes red, sometimes orange in the light. The photographs I'm happiest with, probably because of the festive connection, are of the bird on a whitened branch in a London snow flurry and on a Welsh hillside after heavier snowfall.

When I arrived in mid-Wales in December 2017 to take photos of the valleys thick with white, the steep road down to my family's home was impassable. So I parked my car up on the bank and plunged into the fields with my different lenses. The sun was out and the glistening hills fell away towards the Shropshire flats. For me, it was a fairy landscape; for the local farmer whom I met out feeding his animals, it was part of a tough, hard winter. I spotted a Meadow Pipit standing in the snow and took a picture of it in sharp relief against the white, but I couldn't for a while find a Robin to frame in such a fitting setting. Just when I was desperate to see such a common bird, the Welsh Robins proved frustratingly evasive. Finally, though, I found one patient enough for my camera before it flitted away. There is as much satisfaction in photographing a common bird interestingly and engagingly as there is in capturing a rare bird on camera. Not only is there beauty in familiar species, showing them in original ways draws in the eye of the observer.

above left: Robin,
Notting Hill, London

above right: Robin,
Kensington Gardens, London

CHAFFINCH (14.5cm)

Among our most abundant species, the Chaffinch should not be dismissed. The female *is* admittedly rather drab, but caught in the right light, the male can be a rich mix of russet-pinks and slate grey blue with a flash of green on the wing. They have been reliable residents in our Welsh valley, although I'm writing this profile in August, looking out over a drizzly landscape at the end of a heatwave, and birds in general tend to be more reclusive at this time of year. Some have, according to my knowledgeable local friend and bird recorder, Mike, been filling themselves up in July and are now heading south. Others are enjoying the plentiful supply of early blackberries, damsons and apples, and, less mobile on account of their moulting feathers, are confining themselves to the depths of the hedgerows and the canopies of the trees that are swollen with summer.

One of my most successful shots of a male Chaffinch was from a hide at Lake Vyrnwy. Although I was shooting through the glass, I emerged with a clear image of a bird whose burnt pink breast complemented the browns and golds of the background. Back in England during an Oxfordshire spring, I photographed another male, upright and bearing its tummy to me on the prettiest, lichen-tainted branch of a blackthorn in bloom. Just as backgrounds matter in bird photography, so does the furniture of a shot – in this case a fortuitously pretty bush decorated with white blossom. My image is alive with the colours of spring and the Chaffinch embellishes a picturesque scene.

Look for a glimpse of streaky white on the wing in airborne birds and listen for its throaty song from a perch. Keep an eye out, also, for a Brambling hidden amidst a flock of Chaffinches during the winter. I've only ever seen one in Switzerland, but they are fairly well distributed across the UK in the colder months. You'll notice the black head and wings of the stunning male and the prominent white rumps of both sexes in flight.

Chaffinches themselves are easy to overlook. As a bird photographer – even as a birdwatcher – the temptation is to ignore the more common birds in favour of rarer species. This would be a mistake. The male Chaffinch can be surprisingly photogenic if you bother to pay him attention. Catch him in the right light and he is a sight to behold – and to photograph! If we are prepared to look closely at the birds with which we share our everyday lives, the world can open up to us in exciting ways.

There is even beauty in the greys and browns of the House Sparrow, another of our most familiar birds. When I was growing up in London, before the species suffered a serious decline, the streaky chatterbox was a noisy urban companion and I associate it with hot summer days in the city. Happily, House Sparrows now compete for our attention with Chaffinches on a neighbouring property down the lane in Wales and they nested in our eves one summer after the House Martins had abandoned us.

Chaffinch, Otmoor, Oxfordshire

BULLFINCH (14.5-16.5cm)

There are some birds which reach out beyond the birdwatching community and touch the hearts and imaginations of nature-lovers more generally. I suspect the Bullfinch may be one. Certainly my mother has a special fondness for the male with its bulky red chest and tummy. A mere flash in the hedgerow is usually all you need to identify the bird, whose cap and cheeks are pitch black.

The female's underparts are pale peach-grey, rather than red, but she still cuts a dash with her conspicuous white rump as she bobs between the bushes with her husband. The birds are often seen as a pair, and their flightpath, one following the other, is an endearing, though disappointingly infrequent, trademark of the countryside. Their vegetarian diet consists largely of seeds and the buds of fruit trees, so look out for them in gardens too.

I once struck lucky on the front lawn of my parents' house in Wales. Searching, no doubt, for a snack, a male bird was fidgeting in the grass. I photographed the handsome fellow dressed in a deep orange-red and with a white flower in its beak, as it gave a very passable impression of doing a spot of gardening. A rare and unusual encounter and one I'm glad I memorialised with my camera.

above: Bullfinch, Powys, Mid Wales

opposite: Greenfinch, Lake Vyrnwy, Mid Wales

GREENFINCH (15cm)

The British Greenfinch population has yo-yoed. Having bounced back in the 1990s, it sadly has been in recent decline. The RSPB links the downward trend to an outbreak of trichomonosis, a parasite-induced disease which interferes with birds' ability to feed. The disease, which has also seemed to affect the Chaffinch population, is spread by saliva from infected individuals but the BTO recommends good garden hygiene – such as the regular cleaning and disinfecting of bird tables, bird baths and hanging feeders – as helpful in containing the problem.

Let's hope the Greenfinch makes another recovery, because this is one of our prettiest birds, dressed in an understated green with a grey cheek and yellow streaks on the wings and tail. Less bulky-looking than the Bullfinch, but marginally heavier, the Greenfinch is a solid specimen with a large beak that resembles

a double-sided anvil and with which it can strip the seeds of varying size that comprise its diet. Despite diminished numbers, a pair has been visiting my mother's London feeder regularly. I can't have seen the species more than a dozen or so times, but I photographed a particularly smart example, as it fed at a familiar Lake Vyrnwy hide in Mid Wales.

Birdwatching and bird photography seem, by and large, to be hobbies that people turn to in their more advanced years and my companions in bird hides are almost always considerably older than me. There is no reason, though, why many more children shouldn't get excited about the beauty that graces our gardens and parks. I was a member of the Young Ornithologist's Club, formerly the youth wing of the RSPB, and I fully intend to take my children, if I have them, birdwatching with me.

GREAT SPOTTED WOODPECKER (22-23cm)

The Great Spotted Woodpecker is an old friend from my childhood. A bird often heard before it's seen, this is a species painted boldly in red, white and black. Look out for its bouncing flight and listen for the drumming sound male birds make during springtime as they mark their territory. You may also hear woodpeckers tapping repetitively on wood in search of insects, or in the process of creating a nest hole. I sat patiently at the bird table of a neighbour in Wales, with my long lens balancing on my knee, in the hope that one of the local woodpeckers would put in an appearance. Sure enough, a lovely looking bird came to feed, and I photographed it against the green light of a hot summer's day. At least one of these woodpeckers visited my parents' London garden when I was growing up and much more recently a handsome specimen was only just out of range of a sharp shot in Richmond Park. The male has a flash of red at the back of its head that the female lacks.

The **Green Woodpecker (30-34cm)** is noticeably bigger than the Great Spotted with a less exaggerated, undulating flight and was also a visitor to my parents' communal garden during my childhood. I photographed one looking for worms in Kew Gardens in the autumn of 2018 when I was out searching – unsuccessfully – for the Golden Pheasants that, I'd learned from the Instagram feed of a close friend, had made the beauty spot their home. These woodpeckers are often to be seen feeding on the ground and I finally managed to capture the bird in one of the pools of sunlight afforded by a gap in the trees. Distinctive with its red crown, black face mask, green wings, pale chest and yellow rump, the Green Woodpecker isn't exactly pretty up close but it is striking. The male has an extra sliver of red on the sides of its chin.

left: Green Woodpecker, Kew Gardens, London

opposite: Great Spotted Woodpecker, Powys, Mid Wales

overleaf left (page 36): Blackbird, Buckinghamshire

overleaf right (page 37): Ring-necked Parakeet, Kensington Gardens, London

BLACKBIRD (24-25cm)

You may not need to use your ears to identify a Blackbird in the garden, but so sweet is its song that one of our most familiar birds also offers up one of the most delightful soundtracks to summer. The melodious tune transports me back to warm, sunny, boyhood evenings when the chestnut trees were flush with green. The Beatles, too, recognised its charms. "Blackbird singing in the dead of night" is a line that will never leave me and refers simply but poetically to the dawn chorus, one of nature's most generous gifts.

Most of us are surely at almost constant risk of taking everyday beauty for granted, and a very good example of what I suspect we often overlook, is the contrast between the male Blackbird's smart black plumage and its bright ochre-yellow beak. Look closely at this bird and you'll find a straightforward elegance in its shape as it adorns a garden bush or tree, while hesitating for a moment before departing in a hurry. It's so easy to dismiss what surrounds us, and there is so much pleasure in recognising and acknowledging our neighbours in nature.

The RSPB puts the number of breeding British Blackbirds at more than five million pairs, with 10-15 million birds wintering here from abroad. The species is present all year round across virtually the whole of the UK, so keep an ear out for its song in landscapes as diverse as woodland, farmland and heaths, as well, of course, as in front and back gardens, where you have a good chance of spotting the bird clutching a worm in its beak.

RING-NECKED PARAKEET (38-42cm)

I still meet people who are surprised to see these luminous green, tropical-looking birds in London, but the truth is they are now very common in the capital. In fact, if you're ever in Wormwood Scrubs as the dusk gathers, you may find hundreds, possibly thousands, roosting in the trees. As the sun sets, gangs of these naturalised parrots zip through the streets on their way home to sleep. They're gone in a flash so you may just hear them without laying eyes on the dynamic shapes they make in flight.

I photographed one on a sunlit spring afternoon in Kensington Gardens as it stripped the pink flowers from a horse chestnut tree. A blossom thief! A concerto of colours with a thick red-pink beak, red-rimmed blue eye, and a pink ring around the neck, it made for a pretty picture amid the petals, and its bright green plumage was in sync with the lush foliage.

These noisy invaders, which first became established in the wild during the 1970s after captive birds either escaped or were released, have now fanned out beyond the M25 and M2 and are said to have even reached Scotland. Sadly, they have their enemies, as it's thought they are a potential threat to both crops and native birds. There's even been talk of a cull, but whatever measures government takes, these brightly clad birds, whose origins lie in Africa and lowland India – south of the Himalayas – are here to stay. There's no doubt they add a dash of colour and more than a hint of exoticism to the urban landscape.

WOOD PIGEON (40-42cm)

The nostalgic cooing of the Wood Pigeon is a familiar and reassuring sound on a summer's evening. They would call from the chestnut tree that towered over our back garden when I was a boy. The blue-grey of the head merges into a sky blue before meeting a white neck-scarf that itself sits above a violet chest and grey wings. The beak is orange and pink, the eye black and white. Look closely at this common bird – the RSPB puts their number at nearly five and a half million pairs – and its subtle beauty is obvious. Prominent across most of the country, Wood Pigeons seem equally at home in our gardens and in the fields and woods of our rural landscapes. I've even photographed a bird stealing blossom from a tree on the corner of a busy London street on a warm spring evening. Oh, and don't dismiss the **Feral Pigeon (31-34cm)**, either. Familiar though they are, pay attention and there is not just great variety between individuals but also within the features of a single bird. The shades of green and purple on the neck of the pigeon I photographed up close in Hampstead Heath were an unusual combination and were offset against the orange eye. Another example of everyday beauty in an urban landscape.

below: Feral Pigeon, Hampstead Heath, London

opposite: Wood Pigeon, Richmond Park, London

MAGPIE (44-46cm)

When I was younger, one bird lover I knew revealed to me his desire to shoot magpies. I was appalled. He felt it would have been justified in order to preserve the smaller birds, the eggs and young of which Magpies are known to predate in the spring while they are feeding their own chicks. It is, in fact, legal to trap this species in the UK under a licence and, although I don't instinctively support such a draconian response, particularly given that opinions are said to vary on the extent of damage Magpies do to their nesting neighbours, nevertheless I must confess to irritation and resentment now when I see these instantly recognisable scavengers on the fringes of my parents' Welsh garden. The idea that they might be stripping our local area of even a fraction of its birdlife is a difficult one to stomach. They can also be noisy, aggressive-sounding birds. And then there's my frustrating compulsion to utter words to the effect of "Hello Mr Magpie. How's your wife and children?" whenever I see a single bird. I'm not sure why the superstition, or my corrupted version of it, assumes each Magpie to be a male but I never let a lone bird pass without religiously reciting the greeting.

Still, despite these drawbacks, if you look closely at Magpies, there is lots to admire in their striking black, white, blue and green plumage. When their tail and wing feathers catch the sunlight, they can even lay claim to being a beautiful species. And of course they can't be held morally accountable for the damage they do!

above and opposite: Magpie, Holland Park, London

Countryside Birds

I t's so easy to take the British countryside for granted. Instead, why not revel in its beauty and proximity? If you're a Londoner like me, you don't have to head for the Scottish Highlands to immerse yourself in stunning landscapes. The Welsh hills are three hours away. Even closer are the fields and hedgerows of Buckinghamshire and Oxfordshire. And where there is countryside, there are birds. Sometimes fewer than you might expect – as we'll see in the next chapter, water plays an important role in nourishing birdlife – but it is always worth keeping your eyes peeled and ears pricked for telltale signs of activity. An afternoon out birdwatching in the country can be re-energising – and good for the waistline too!

Wherever you live or travel to in the country, there will be many species to discover and, if you catch the bug, to photograph. But don't make the mistake of ignoring common birds. Look closely and they can reveal astonishing beauty. Take the **Pheasant (53-89cm)** pictured opposite, for example. Isn't he marvellous? I was out taking pictures of rarer species when he caught my eye with his bright red face, blue-green neck and russet waistcoat.

The Welsh hills, with their nooks and crannies, are particularly special to me and, although I can't escape to them as often as I was once able to, I still visit at least four or five times a year. Resident Buzzards hunt the valley in front of my parents' house and a Goshawk – a bird I still long to see for the first time – once nested in nearby woods. Red Kites are occasional visitors and Tawny Owls call out to one another after dark. Pied Flycatchers visit the tree-lined lanes in spring and my mother spent warm, sunny afternoons watching a Spotted Flycatcher feeding its young in the garden one summer not so long ago. House Martins used to make their homes in the eaves and Grey Wagtails occasionally wag their tails on the slate roof. Linnets, Bullfinches, and tiny Wrens and Goldcrests are all to be found in our local area, too, and I spotted and photographed my first Garden Warbler on the edge of local woodland.

Pheasant, Otmoor, Oxfordshire

As children, my brothers and I would spend many weeks of our holidays in Mid Wales and the spirit of the place runs deep in my soul. The primroses on the banks in April, the long summer evenings, the first chill of an autumn mist, and the warmth of the log fire in winter – these are formative memories. I find myself craving the place when I've been away too long and when I am there, I try to throw myself out into the fields rather than stay in doors, glued to a screen. Badgers forage and foxes hunt close to the house, and weasels sneak across the hillsides. And while there isn't much water around beyond the stream at the foot of the valley, the bird life is rich – so long as you listen and look!

Stonechat, Pembrokeshire

STONECHAT (12.5cm)

The Stonechat has become a familiar companion as I walk the English and Welsh countryside with camera in hand. I don't often, though, give them the attention their pretty colouring deserves, as I press on in search of rarer species. The adult male, a bird I've never photographed satisfactorily, sports a gorgeous black cape, an orange breast, and a bright white collar. The female, as is often the case in the avian world, is more muted in her plumage.

When I do stop to pay attention to one of these elegant little birds, they can remain tantalisingly out of range. One of the prettiest pictures I've taken stars a female or juvenile bird balancing almost impossibly on the fringe of a bracken frond, backlit and in sumptuous collaboration with the golden oranges and browns of a sunny autumn day in Richmond Park. Sadly the photograph is insufficiently sharp to appear in the pages of this book, and I still regret having been unable to draw closer.

I hope in my photographs to draw the eye in an unfussy way to the beauty of birds, but it is always exciting to capture a species actually *doing* something. Although also marginally too 'soft' to reproduce here, I posted on Instagram a dramatic 'action' shot of another Stonechat, this time a native of Essex, launching itself skywards from a rusty pole near Clacton-on-Sea. It had caught my eye while I was photographing a vagrant Rough-legged Buzzard and, while tiny by comparison, produced a comic image of take-off, Stonechat-style.

Finally, although my search for a pleasing shot of a male Stonechat in full adult plumage goes on, I did photograph what appeared to be a first year male that performed for me close at hand during a cliff-top walk along the Pembrokeshire coast on a summer's evening. I probably spent twenty minutes distracted by this more muted bird and captured it singing from the top of a bright purple foxglove.

Listen for the Stonechat's grating call – it really does sound like two stones being chafed together – and look out for the flicking of wings as it clings to a fond or stem. Just be careful, depending on where you are in the country, not to confuse the bird with the similar looking, though scarcer and non-resident, Whinchat.

I have happy memories of walking the Berwyn Hills of Mid Wales as a boy and watching as a Stonechat or Whinchat would rise up from the bracken. Every so often, a **Wheatear (14.5cm)** would make an appearance too. Slightly larger than either species, Wheatears are summer visitors that breed in western and northern Britain, and in smaller numbers in the south and east. The species is also a passage migrant which means that birds may stop off here to refuel during migration. The male is grey on top, with dark wings and eye-stripe and a flash of white on its rump. They mainly live on the ground and you'll see them hopping along the landscape and pausing, seemingly for thought, on a stone or rock. I got lucky with both colour and composition when I photographed the bird on a Pembrokeshire headland. What a beauty it was!

SEDGE WARBLER (13cm)

On a sunny summer's day in 2011, I found myself in the East Riding of Yorkshire to film the seabirds that cram the chalk-white Bempton Cliffs for my BBC documentary about the RSPB's Conservation Director and author of the foreword to this book, Martin Harper. Gannets glided in and out, Kittiwakes, Fulmars, Razorbills and Guillemots were there in huge numbers, and Puffins cleaved to the rock face. This frantic activity adds up to one of the great spectacles of British wildlife. But a highlight of the day for me was the vigorous little Sedge Warbler that clung to a reed and waved about in the wind as it sang its busy song. Summer visitors from sub-Saharan Africa, these warblers are mimics and can weave the notes of other birds into their music.

Years later, and after several failed attempts, I photographed a Sedge Warbler singing from another reed, two hundred miles south, at RSPB Otmoor. The dark bushes behind the bird were set far enough back to create a lovely, dappled green effect; the orange from inside its musical mouth contrasted prettily with the smooth white of the chest and underbelly.

Sedge Warblers are energetic birds and they like wet habitats. They are present in much of the British Isles during the warmer months of the year and the prominent white eye-stripe helps to distinguish the species from the buffer but no less beautiful **Reed Warbler (13cm).**

Reed Warblers are more shy in their behaviour than Sedge – and only half as many birds visit our shores in summer, according to the RSPB – but I captured one with my lens on the banks of a waterway at the same Oxfordshire reserve: a small, delicately drawn bird, turned pale gold as it emerged into the sunshine from the matching colours of the reedbed in which it had been hiding. Slightly larger, and from another family altogether, is the Reed Bunting. A common bird, you may catch it flying through the reedbeds or even, as I once photographed a male, with its prominent black head, tucked away in the pussy willow of an English spring.

Unlike Sedge and Reed Warblers, Dartford Warblers can be seen throughout the year in Britain, although there are far fewer of them. These are gorgeous birds, with their long, cocked tails, blue-grey heads and, in the case of the male, a deep wine-red chest. I photographed them on a hot, sunny day on Hengistbury Head on the fringes of Bournemouth and overlooking the Isle of Wight, but I've also heard them closer to home in Thursley Common. I had stood little chance of seeing a Dartford Warbler in childhood because, as with many of our rarer birds, they are largely confined to specific areas, so I was thrilled to see them for the first time in my mid-thirties. You have to be prepared to travel if you want to broaden the scope of your birdwatching, but with effort so often comes reward!

left: Reed Warbler,
Otmoor, Oxfordshire

opposite: Sedge Warbler,
Otmoor, Oxfordshire

LINNET (13.5cm)

Sadly there are far fewer of these pretty finches than their once were in the UK and their population is estimated to have dropped by over half between 1970 and 2014. Many of our bird species have suffered similarly and primarily as a result of habitat loss. Not to be mistaken for the Redpoll, male Linnets have a crimson dash on their foreheads and chests. In summer you may see them on heathland flitting from bush to bush; in winter they can gather into flocks and move, as one, in undulating flight, calling as they fly.

As is so often the case with bird photography, trying to capture a Linnet before it darts off noisily can be a frustrating experience. They regularly abandon their perch just as you make a final approach. I've played catch-up with Linnets on a Pembrokeshire headland and photographed them at Otmoor where one did sit still for long enough to afford an arresting portrait against a background of greens and yellows in layered harmony.

WHITETHROAT (14cm)

Looking for the resident Short-eared Owls on Skomer Island during a memorable afternoon photographing Puffins, I stumbled upon a Whitethroat, posing briefly on a thin branch. Like the Linnet I snapped in Oxfordshire, the bird stood out from a gorgeous backdrop, only this time, the image was blessed with a purple haze. Luck is an indispensable assistant of the bird photographer.

Whitethroats have smart white necks, grey heads, chestnut wing feathers and a long tail. They belong to the warbler family and join us each summer from sub-Saharan Africa. It is mind-boggling to think that a bird no bigger than a Great Tit can travel so far. The species breeds across much of the UK and more widely than the smaller Lesser Whitethroat.

opposite: Whitethroat,
Skomer Island, Pembrokeshire

right: Linnet, Otmoor, Oxfordshire

NUTHATCH (14cm)

Unlike the Treecreeper, Nuthatches can climb both up and down a tree. Treecreepers can only climb upwards (unless they hop down backwards to avoid their tail getting in the way) so when they reach the top of a trunk they often fly back down to the bottom to begin again their search for insects and spiders. Treecreepers are pretty in their porcelain way with thin and elegantly curved beaks, bright white underparts and mottled brown wings and head. But they are not so bold in their beauty as the spectacular Nuthatch with its blue-grey top, black eye-stripe, white chin and orange chest and tummy. I have successfully photographed one of these handsome birds through the glass of an RSPB hide at Lake Vyrnwy, but I've never managed the right angle, nor timed my shot quite right, at the bird-feeders of our neighbours in Mid Wales.

above: Nuthatch, Lake Vyrnwy, Mid Wales

opposite: Meadow Pipit, Iceland

overleaf left (page 52): Skylark, Pembrokeshire

overleaf right (page 53): Rock Pipit, Pembrokeshire

MEADOW PIPIT (14.5cm)

The Meadow Pipit's fluttering parachute display flight in the warmer months shouldn't be mistaken for that of the more illustrious **Skylark (18-19cm)**, which ascends directly heavenward in a manner made famous in the stories of our childhood. The Skylark, a species given special protection under Schedule 1 of the Wildlife and Countryside Act 1981, is umbilically linked in my imagination to the English summer, but the Meadow Pipit is also an attractive presence. Note the white fringes to its airborne wings, and listen out for a repetitive tweeting as it flies.

I've photographed the Meadow Pipit, surrounded by greens and purples, during a Pembrokeshire summer (see page 8) and captured it in winter, too, sunlit in the Mid Welsh snow. I took my most successful picture of the species, however, in another part of the world entirely. I was out on the moors in Iceland searching for water birds on a grey lake, our 4x4 parked up on the edge of the road, when I spotted the familiar shape of an elegant pipit standing on the edge of a boulder. Something about the soft light, the composition and the out-of-focus background make this one of my favourite photos of any bird. Normally I like to crop my images to reveal the intricate patterns and interweaving colours of plumage. Here, though, I wanted to allow the crispness of the bird in its setting of gentle rustic colours to make its own statement.

Although the larger **Rock Pipit (16.5cm)** is a duller bird with darker legs than its Meadow counterpart, get lucky with a background that mirrors its colouring and the species can be the centrepiece of an aesthetically pleasing image. I've photographed several birds perched on rocks on the Pembrokeshire coast after playing protracted games of hide-and-seek with them. The challenge is, as so often, to edge close enough along the pebbled shore before the pipit loses confidence and hurries off, sometimes stirring up other birds that you hadn't even noticed in its frenzied dash for a 'safer' distance. What's frustrating is that it almost always makes its move just as you approach to within perfect range. Still, if photographing birds were easy, some of the fun – as well as the reward – would be stripped away, and I've returned to the same beach in the hope of improving my results.

YELLOWHAMMER (16-16.5cm)

The head feathers of the male Yellowhammer are almost luridly yellow. One of my first sightings of the species was at close range on a hot English afternoon in the late spring of 2014, on the outskirts of Salisbury. As part of the 'portfolio' presenting career I have developed since leaving the BBC the previous year, I regularly host events on stage, many of them at literary festivals that fan out across England – from Oxford to Harrogate via Hay. One of my favourite venues is the Salisbury Playhouse, with its soft lighting and deep pink seating, and I've interviewed many famous names there as part of the Salisbury International Arts Festival.

There is a particular buzz to performing in front of a live audience, but the excitement of my stints in Salisbury has not been confined to its theatre. In between interviewing John Cleese or Rory Bremner, I like to drive out into the Wiltshire or Dorset countryside in search of landscapes and birds to photograph. Right on the edge of the city lies the Iron Age hill fort of Old Sarum. The ruins afford glorious views of the the famous cathedral and, as I discovered during my first week at the festival, they are also home to the Yellowhammer's distinctive and persistent song in spring. Finding the brightly coloured bird in these surroundings was a particular joy because, when I was a boy, our Christmases and Easters on the secular Jewish side of my family (the older generation of which escaped the Nazi seizure of Vienna in the 1930s), would often be hosted in Salisbury, and I used to clamber up and down the chalk slopes of a moat that encircles the fort.

The male Yellowhammer is immediately recognisable thanks to its garish yellow head and underparts, and its chestnut rump is also a standout feature. The female's colouring is less raucous. You'll see these residents singing from a perch, or maybe foraging for seeds left out on the ground. The photograph of the species I took in Salisbury is bold but marginally blurred – and 'marginally' is enough to ruin a photo – because my lens focused on the foliage of the hedgerow in front of the bird. Instead, the male pictured on the opposite page is one I found at RSPB Otmoor, where it was posing proudly among the April blackthorn blossom.

Yellowhammer, Otmoor, Oxfordshire

SNOW BUNTING (16-17cm)

I met Anna at the Salisbury International Arts Festival in 2014. She was exhibiting her photographs of the Eyjafjallajökull volcanic activity that had caused so many international flights to be grounded in 2010. I was in town to interview celebrities and lesser known writers on stage as part of a collaboration between the festival and *The Telegraph*, for which I was a regular interviewer. I wrote a daily blog for the paper, too, and interviewed Anna on a sunlit drive to Old Wardour Castle where Shakespeare's *Much Ado About Nothing* was being staged in the open air. It was one of those golden early summer evenings that the English countryside does so well and the Dorset landscape was in full cry.

Anna took me back in time to the ash cloud which she braved in order to document the destructive force of the erupting volcano. "We had to have masks on, we had to have glasses, because the dust is so fine it goes into your system even if you don't breathe," she told me. "And it's dangerous. When we were there in the cloud it was really, really scary. And then you stopped thinking about it because you started photographing." That moment when thought stops and photography takes over is so familiar to me as a bird photographer. I've waded recklessly through snake territory to sneak closer to my subject. (Please don't follow my example!)

Three years after Anna told me her story, I headed to the airport from Leicester Square, where I had just finished broadcasting to the nation's night workers and insomniacs, and boarded a plane to Reykjavik.

Later that morning I touched down, bleary-eyed but excited, and was met by my new friend.

Anna showed me her Arctic island with the enthusiasm of a fellow photographer. In between pointing my camera at the mighty waterfalls and majestic glaciers, we kept an eye out for Iceland's birdlife. From Harlequin Ducks to Whooper Swans, the endemic species were impressive though not extensive. And while the eerily beautiful Gyr Falcon and powerful White-tailed Eagles proved predictably elusive, a surprise awaited me in a car park whose primary function is to service the thousands of tourists that gather each year to visit the Jökulsárlón Lagoon.

Flitting from the top of a camper van to the gravelly tarmac, was a male Snow Bunting. I'd seen the similarly coloured Snow Finch while skiing in the Swiss Alps as a teenager but this, I think, was a first for me. Frothy white in its chest – and only fractionally bigger than a Chaffinch – it also alighted, as if just for my lens, on a bright blue roof which matched the sharp blue sky. I managed to photograph this glorious bird as it sang full-throatedly above the eye-line of tourists who were entirely unaware of what they were missing. I even captured it perched by an old wheel, its rusty shoulders mirroring the rusty hub.

Snow Buntings are uncommon residents in Scotland, though you might spot one during the British winter, when they visit much of our coastline. The beaches of North Norfolk, I'm told, are a good place to find them.

opposite above and below:
Snow Bunting, Iceland

COMMON STARLING (21cm)

I don't have a grand story of adventure to tell you about my revelatory encounter with a Starling. I wasn't in a tropical paradise or in a secluded wood on the slopes of a Swiss mountain. I wasn't even in the British countryside. Instead, my eyes were opened to the rainbow glory of a Common Starling in a central London park. And therein lies, I hope, this book's enduring message.

Did you know that Starlings' beaks are black in winter and yellow in the breeding season? I didn't, until I wrote about it here. It would be easy to dismiss these birds as everyday nonentities, but it would also be a mistake. It is not just the more striking beauty of birds such as the rarer – and shier – **Jay (34-35cm)** – that remind us of how special our world is. Look closely at Starlings' plumage in the sunlight and they become illuminated wonders with speckled heads and chests, and hints of green that harmonise with the yolk-yellow summer beak. The bird I photographed at close range as it stood on the edge of the Round Pond in

Kensington Gardens came alive in the glow of the day. The water, on which I floated my red wooden duck as a two-year-old in the early 1980s, now acted as a milky blue backdrop and I was infused with the iridescent beauty of a bird I had for so long overlooked.

If you ever get the chance, make your way to the RSPB's Otmoor reserve during the winter just before sunset and you stand a chance of witnessing one of British wildlife's most gobsmacking sights. I've watched – and photographed – thousands, maybe tens of thousands, of Starlings gather in a noisy murmuration as they prepared to roost for the night. The closely formed groupings are thought to offer a defence against predation from birds of prey but they provide us with an extraordinary display. In Denmark, murmurations more than a million-strong are said to be visible above the Jutland marshlands in the spring. Birds really do have the capacity to amaze, and not just as individuals but as participants in breathtaking choreography.

opposite: Common Starling, Kensington Gardens, London

overleaf: Common Starlings, Otmoor, Oxfordshire

below: Jay, Buckinghamshire

REDWING (21cm)

Watch out for these visitors during the British winter. I seem to remember my birdwatcher uncle telling us when I was a child that a Redwing had visited either his Edinburgh garden or our own. I recall keeping an eye out for the distinctive bird, as a result, with its conspicuous red patches on flank and underwing and the prominent beige-white eyebrows. Decades passed, however, before I could be sure that I had actually seen one. Members of the thrush family, Redwings are marked on their chests and tummies in much the same way as Mistle and Song Thrushes are. I photographed two birds in Iceland, one singing on the edge of a cliff with its black-tipped yellow beak. They were one of the more regular local breeding birds I encountered on a trip that was marked mainly by ruggedly beautiful landscapes.

Migrating Redwings can form parties with the likes of Blackbirds, Song Thrushes and Fieldfares. Although not all Redwings are migratory, those that breed in the far eastern limits of the species' range can fly thousands of kilometres in search of a winter home. Isn't that mind-boggling?

left and opposite: Redwing, Iceland

CHOUGH (39-40cm)

For years, maybe decades, I carried with me the vague notion – more a hope really – that I had laid eyes on these splendid corvids as a boy, but I suspect the line between memory and fantasy had begun to blur by the time I was finally able to say for sure that I'd seen a Chough. I'd watched yellow-beaked Alpine Choughs hang above the heads of skiers in the Swiss Alps, but it wasn't until I walked the Pembrokeshire cliffs near Martin's Haven that I finally spotted, with total certainty, the fabulous red-legged, red-beaked Chough that is native to Britain. And what a bird it is, so obviously different from other members of its family.

If you're on the western fringes of Britain, it's worth checking that what might at first seem to be a Crow isn't, on closer inspection, a Chough. I've now learned to pick out its call and finger-like wing tips, and I've spotted the graceful bird further along the Pembrokeshire cliffs while on holiday with my wife, staying at her grandfather's house. These really are stunning birds, thanks in part to the unexpected splashes of red at their extremities. Which isn't to belittle the magical quality of a parliament of Rooks as they flock forth from a rookery; nor to ignore the startling pale-blue eye of the squat **Jackdaw (34cm)** – a regular of Richmond Park on the outskirts of London – with its wedge-like beak; let alone to dismiss the glory of the Raven, twice a Jackdaw's size, and master of the skies it soars.

above: Choughs, Pembrokeshire   *opposite:* Jackdaw, Richmond Park, London

Water
Birds

As a boy, wandering the hills and fields of Mid Wales, I would grow frustrated by the limits of my lens. Why *were* my binoculars filled with Common Buzzards, Ravens and, if I was lucky, a distant Sparrowhawk? What about Reed Buntings, Merlin and warblers of every kind?

I didn't hit upon the answer until, thanks to the lure of Instagram, I started photographing birds in my mid-thirties. Suddenly it was obvious. Water! If you want to add species to your list or get quite close to rare birds, the nearer you are to water, the more successful you're often likely to be. It's no surprise, therefore, that many of this country's nature reserves, whether they're run by the National Trust, the RSPB, or another organisation, are located on wetlands and or on the coast.

On a single grey October afternoon I saw my first Marsh Harrier *and* Hobby – the latter dipping suddenly and scattering waterfowl as it lunged – at the National Trust Reserve at Cley in Norfolk. Had I been luckier, I might also have spotted a Hen Harrier. Instead I had to wait for my trip to the Fens, themselves fed plentifully by water, and a magical winter's evening at the Wicken Fen reserve. Birds like water. And not just the waders, which tuck into the rich pickings on offer on marsh and wetland. Predators, whether harrier, falcon or hawk, feast on the water birds themselves.

Don't forget, either, the yield of a coastal habitat like Bempton Cliffs, where Gannets, Puffins, Guillemots and Razorbills perform or pose in staggering displays.

Little Egret, Zanzibar, Tanzania

KINGFISHER (16-17cm)

Water, then, is essential if you want to take your birding to another level. You're missing out if you don't journey up and down river, across the sea and onto our lakes and reservoirs. And of all the birds in a British birdwatcher's guidebook, is there another as startlingly sensational as the Kingfisher? Its azure blue and bright orange plumage catches the light like no other, immediately setting it apart. Hard to miss, you might think. Yet I couldn't be sure that I'd seen this tiny fish-guzzler until my mid-thirties when, on a sun-drenched afternoon, Mike, a neighbour in Wales, took my mother and me out in his Land Rover.

We made our way to the riverbank through a field that was turning ochre in the afternoon light. Sand Martins dipped along the water's edge and the distant Berwyn hills framed an idyllic summer view. Puffy clouds seemed to emphasise the perfection of the day.

A keen eye, as much as patience, is an essential companion to the ornithologist. My mother is blessed with the quickest visual reflexes of anyone I've met and has an uncanny knack of picking out wildlife the rest of us miss. And so it was that she was the first to spy the Kingfisher, flashing past in its sparkly feathers. Of course, I was anxious I had missed out! But then, alerted I think by its gentle, understated whistle, my eyes fixed the bird rushing along the river again in a frightful hurry.

Incongruously, the most visually impressive birds can be the least exciting musicians. The Golden Eagle's weak call seems unworthy of its giant frame and the Kingfisher's feeble whistle never turns into song. Equally, the drabbest dressers can perform the most exquisite concertos and symphonies. Think the unspectacular Garden and Cetti's Warblers.

Long though the experience will live in the memory, our sightings of the Kingfisher that Welsh afternoon were typical of many encounters with the bird. That famous flash and it's gone. So, armed with a picnic and accompanied by an indulgent girlfriend (who is now my wife), her best friend, and her younger sister,

I set off one May day from London for the RSPB Rye Meads Nature Reserve in Hertfordshire. Weeks earlier, while watching Ospreys near Machynlleth in the Dovey Estuary, I'd overheard another birder extol the reserve's virtues as a site to photograph the species.

Like the Skylark, for example, the Kingfisher is a Schedule 1 bird which means it is afforded special protections under the law. Photographers and birdwatchers should always prioritise the welfare of any bird, but it is an offence intentionally or recklessly to disturb Schedule 1 species at, on or near an 'active' nest. Fortunately the RSPB at Rye Meads have built a hide at a safe viewing distance from the nest so that the birds are not disturbed.

The reserve itself, on the fringes of a sewage works, is unprepossessing, but soon enough, the familiar fusion of orange and blue appeared across the water. We watched as the bird clasped a tiny fish in its long beak after splashing down below the surface, and although my pictures were disappointing, I have since returned with a more powerful 500mm zoom.

All too often, Kingfishers fall victim to hard winters, and juveniles, as with many species, are also particularly vulnerable in their early weeks. Kingfisher pairs compensate by sometimes parenting two or three broods in a single year, with five to seven eggs typical of a clutch. Parents take it in turn to incubate the eggs and each chick can eat 12-18 fish a day, which is a lot of fishing for mum and dad!

British birds number in their thousands of pairs, but ours is the only one of more than a hundred species of Kingfisher to breed in the UK. And consider this as you marvel at the brilliance of its colouring: the dancing hues of its back owe their brightness not to pigment but to the way light hits the layered feathers – which aren't really blue at all. At least that is *my* understanding of what I've read of the science!

right and overleaf: Kingfisher, Rye Meads, Hertfordshire

left: Grey Wagtail, Powys, Mid Wales

opposite: Atlantic Puffin, Skomer Island, Pembrokeshire

GREY WAGTAIL (18-19cm)

A busy bird, whose name belies its rich yellow underparts. I've traced these water-loving wagtails up and down our local stream in Wales in the hope of managing a sharp shot. Their slate grey heads and black and white facial masks help make this one of Britain's prettiest birds, and I hope one day to take a photograph that does them justice. One morning, from the comfort of my bedroom, I spotted what looked like a family fluttering playfully on the roof. Such a treat to be visited by one of my favourite native species.

ATLANTIC PUFFIN (28-30cm)

Puffins aren't just adorable looking birds, they possess formidable powers of endurance. For the far greater part of the year they are solitary creatures and survive far from land, insulated from the cold by their downy under-plumage. It is thought they are offered some protection from aerial predators by blending into the deep blue sea with their dark overcoats, and from submarine attackers by the white of their fronts mixing with the brightness of the light. During the springtime they leave the ocean and, in a bid to escape foxes and other terrestrial predators, they head mostly to small islands where they begin to build their nests in burrows with their mates.

Normally monogamous, on account, apparently, of their attachment to their burrows, Puffins re-establish their bond through nest-building as well as through 'billing', a ritual that involves the birds approaching each other, wagging their heads from side to side and then rattling their beaks together. Whether or not you're an avid birdwatcher, how could you not have a soft spot for these utterly charming creatures?

Puffins produce a single puffling each year and feed their offspring with the sand eels they catch by propelling themselves forwards underwater with the wings they use as paddles. They are able to spend a whole minute at a time beneath the surface, and their strong, grooved tongues, serrated beaks, and the hinging of their mandibles allow them to gather a cluster of shiny fish during a single expedition.

When I set off for Skomer Island from London in the month of June, I was after that iconic shot of a Puffin with a bill full of sand eels. I'd been warned to arrive early at the ferry's office at Martin's Haven to be sure of making one of the crossings. As it turned out, the boats hadn't been able to run the previous day – it's all about the power and direction of the wind apparently – so I was relieved to have won my place in an already

burgeoning queue by 7.30 in the morning. After successfully buying my ticket, I whiled away the hours before the departure of the third or fourth ferry of the day by photographing Choughs on the peninsular above the terminal.

Skomer itself is a pretty little island off one of the westernmost tips of Wales. Following a brief trip from the mainland during which we were cosily crammed aboard a rudimentary vessel by a cheerful ferryman, we were given four hours in which to make our way criss-crossing up and down its gentle undulations. Oystercatchers and aggressive gulls lined my path as I headed for the famous Wick where the Puffins congregate in their greatest numbers. Once there, you have to take care not to trip over the surprisingly little birds as they hurry across the path.

The Puffins stood in pairs outside their burrows or gathered in little conferences on the cliff's edge. Above our heads, hundreds wheeled back and forth, some aborting their landings at the last moment, others coming in to land awkwardly and at ferocious pace. One or two seemed to miss their holes. Almost all were too fast for me, although I did at least manage one shot of a bird in flight with a mouthful of sand eels and another, without fish, on the point of touchdown.

On land, however, the Puffins presented tame targets for the photographer. That said, I wish I'd taken longer to photograph those birds whose colourful beaks were stuffed full of glinting fish. One of my pictures made it into *The Times* as photograph of the day. I did also capture one Puffin – a late arrival perhaps – preparing to line its nest with grass, and some of the birds I photographed were beautifully offset by colourful backgrounds of bottle or lime greens. I certainly didn't regret the demanding, one night stay, six hundred mile round trip, and I shall have to return another year.

Skomer is an avian paradise that is also at the centre of a good news story. While Puffin populations have generally been struggling in Europe, the birds on this tiny isle, protected by The Wildlife Trust of South & West Wales, have been thriving and their numbers have almost quadrupled over the past 30 years or so. Long may the good work continue, because, while there are still hundreds of thousands of breeding pairs in British colonies, RSPB scientists have warned that the species could become extinct.

above, opposite and overleaf: Atlantic Puffin, Skomer Island, Pembrokeshire

ARCTIC TERN (33-36cm)

Arctic Terns are by no means confined to the Arctic. You'll find them breeding on the Farne Islands in Northumberland, for example, and it's worth keeping an eye out for them on spring passage at inland reservoirs and in coastal areas during the autumn as they fly south. Their northern range stretches east across Siberia and west to the Alaskan shore. I have yet to encounter these noisy birds here, but I feasted my eyes on a colony in Iceland, having driven about 230 miles east from Reykjavik along the southern shore of the island. We found them in a frenzied grouping around the Breiðamerkurjökull glacier that ends in the Jökulsárlón lagoon.

Arctic Terns experience two summers each year as they migrate, astonishingly, between the Arctic and the Antarctic. In 2016, one of these remarkable travellers notched up the longest migration ever recorded during its round-trip between the Farne Islands and Antarctica. Stopping to fish along the way, the bird journeyed a mind-boggling 59,650 miles, which amounts to more than twice the circumference of the Earth. At least, though, it took time to enjoy the view. The Bar-tailed Godwit can fly from the Arctic to New Zealand in just eight days, without pausing to refuel. Wow.

With their aerodynamic heads and silver wings, Arctic Terns seem to cut through the air. There was nothing elegant, however, about the deafening din they produced, as I watched them shouting and quarrelling in great numbers over fish. With the glacier before me and the sea behind, I watched as these boisterous locals competed in great numbers for congested airspace, or stopped to rest on a crowded, grassy stretch. In such circumstances, I shoot as much as I can, hoping for a little luck as I train my lens on the birds in flight and with fish in their mouths. This is where a sizeable memory card is essential – you don't want to run out of film as you witness one of nature's unfolding spectacles! What is it they say about about luck lurking where opportunity meets preparation?

That sunny Icelandic afternoon, I was *really* lucky. Amongst the hundreds of shots I took, one stood out. Not only did the Arctic Tern hold a silver fish in its beak – the eye of both the bird and its catch in focus – the activity was offset by a gorgeously muted backdrop of red, orange and pink. Entirely unintentional. Hugely gratifying. I also captured birds on the ground, squawking loudly and vying for attention with their red beaks prominent against the green of a knoll.

Arctic Terns are thought to reach up to 30 years of age, and it is somehow comforting to think of these incredible piscators returning each year to their breeding colonies, having ventured so many thousands of miles in the process. Giant swallows of the deep, these agile masters of the air will, with a fair wind, be fishing the icy waters of the Arctic for centuries to come.

left and opposite: Arctic Tern, Iceland

BLACK-HEADED GULL (34-37cm)

Just because they're a common sight – according to the RSPB, more than two million birds winter here and there are 140,000 breeding pairs – it doesn't mean these gulls aren't worth studying closely with their brown heads (which turn white outside the summer months) and red beaks and legs. Before I caught the bug of bird photography, I took pictures of Black-headed Gulls on a sunlit day one Christmas, as they stood on a frozen Round Pond in London's Kensington Gardens. An image that I took of a bird causing ripples in the pond's surface in warmer times helped illustrate the article I wrote about birdwatching for *The Telegraph* in 2015. "I'm a birdwatcher and I'm not afraid to admit it", ran the headline. But the best shot I've taken of this species was more recently, while watching Sandwich Terns fishing off the coast of Brownsea Island in Dorset. In the edit, I zoomed in on the face and a drop of water caught the light as it fell from the tip of a glistening beak. Expect these birds inland as well as on the coast.

top: Black-headed Gull, Brownsea Island, Dorset

above: Black-headed Gull, Kensington Gardens, London

opposite: Sandwich Tern, Brownsea Island, Dorset

SANDWICH TERN (36-41cm)

There are some British birds you are unlikely to see unless you make the effort to find them on a map. The Sandwich Terns of Brownsea Island live together on a crowded bit of land that juts out from the lagoon in Poole Harbour. Like their Arctic cousins, they make a racket as they squabble and play together, seemingly taunting one another with a recent catch of sand eel. Young birds mingle with their more striking parents, uncles and aunts, waiting for a fish.

I set off in search of them – and the red squirrels with which they share the island – on a sunny morning in July. Small ferries were departing from Poole throughout much of the day and I was soon walking the coastal path towards the hide which stands almost on top of the terns' nesting station. On the way, I spotted in the distance my first Spoonbills, feeding in the silt on their ungainly legs, or maybe just enjoying the good weather. Then I was among the Sandwich Terns, some preening themselves on wooden poles that studded the shallow water, others frenziedly flying to and fro with a fish in their beaks.

Smart in their black, white and grey with an impressive crest, Sandwich Terns can resemble a rather pompous Rear Admiral kitted out for sea. They are also the punk-rockers of British Terns, impossible to miss with their tufted hairstyles. Prominent, too, are the yellow tips to their powerful black beaks. Some have a downy white on their otherwise coal black crowns, but their eyes are swallowed by the dark plumage and this can make life tricky for the bird photographer because the test of a competent picture is whether the eye is in focus.

Water birds, though, are often the easiest to snap because they have already found what they're looking for in their native lagoon or estuary and are less likely to fly off in search of alternative feeding locations. Locating Sandwich Terns is also helped by the fact that British colonies are often reliant on nature reserves for their survival. I had my pick of these birds as they took it in turns(!) to dart here and there before my lens. The challenge, though, was – as with the Arctic Terns – not simply to take a perfectly sharp image but to photograph one with a freshly caught fish wedged in its beak.

The protective wiring with which the National Trust has enclosed the terns' roosting area can ruin a photograph, but there are ample opportunities for clean shots when the birds are airborne. I emerged with a favourite image that cast the tern as an angel of the sea with its wings tilted heavenwards and its head pointed down towards the water. Oh, and I also managed to spot and photograph the most famous of the island's inhabitants: the red squirrel. (Although not bounding from branch to branch as I'd hoped!).

opposite and above: Sandwich Tern,
Brownsea Island, Dorset

left: Whimbrel, Iceland

below: Oystercatcher, Skomer Island, Pembrokeshire

WHIMBREL (40-46cm)

The Whimbrel is a rare bird in the UK and only breeds in northern Scotland, although you might catch one passing through elsewhere in the spring or autumn. Be careful not to confuse it with the similar looking but larger and far more populous Curlew, of which there are said by the RSPB to be 66,000 breeding pairs in Britain (compared to just 400-500 Whimbrel couples). I can't be sure whether I have ever seen a Whimbrel here but I photographed one running across an Icelandic moor. There's a wistful quality to the bird in the picture as it turns to look at me with its long, gently curved beak. The wattled brown and white of its head and back are almost camouflaged in the bleak beiges of the Arctic island landscape as it hurries on its way. Although you will find these birds wading for small crabs on the coast, they breed on moorland. Listen for the song that grows quickly to a frenetic whistle.

Iceland doesn't have a long species list, but those birds that do make the island their home are well worth spending time with. The same moor that produced the running Whimbrel also yielded a Ptarmigan (34-36cm) in its white winter plumage. In Britain, these stunning birds breed in the highest mountains of the Highlands and form part of the Golden Eagle's diet. I photographed the bird launching itself from a mossy rock, its red eyebrow prominent above the black beak. Controversially, Ptarmigan is a popular festive meat in Iceland. Although hunting the species was banned on the island in 2003-4 in deference to a decline in its population, the practice seems to have been lawful again since 2005 on selected days which are determined annually.

Not far from the Ptarmigan, we had earlier almost literally bumped into a **Golden Plover (26-29 cm)**, regal in its summer feathers of dappled gold, with a smart black face and chest fringed with white, and standing fearlessly in the middle of the road. I've photographed these lovely birds in their hundreds, possibly thousands, flocking above the wetlands at RSPB Otmoor in their shimmering colours. **Oystercatchers (40-45cm)** were in the area as well,

although I've taken my best shots of these stand-out black and white waders on Skomer Island in Wales. The orange-red beaks with which they catch cockles and mussels on the coast – and worms inland – are eye-catching.

Excitingly, I saw my first **Harlequin Ducks (36-51cm)** and **Common Eider (50-71cm)** in Iceland. I spotted a pair of the former from the road on a river not far from the sea and photographed the male with its navy blue head that boasts white markings, a rufous streak and a black bar running along the crown. I would like to have captured its face close-up in all its unusual intricacy but my wide shot took in the moist boulders that protruded from the sparkling water. The perculiar-looking Eider I framed as it flew in to land on the icy waters of a glacial lake, its black-edged wings anchoring the white body and its yellow beak jutting forward. As with Sandwich Terns, the eye of the Eider, which is the largest duck in Europe and one of Britain's fastest flying birds, is buried in black facial feathers, which makes capturing its personality more of a challenge.

Eiders dive for crustaceans and molluscs and are said to have a particularly soft spot for mussels, which they swallow in their entirety before the shells are crushed in their gizzard and excreted. Crabs, however, have their claws and legs stripped before they are consumed. True to their diet, Eiders live in coastal areas, and the Farne Islands are reputably a good spot to see them. They're sociable ducks and females often share parenting duties with other hens.

Altogether more beautiful than the Eider were the Black-throated Divers – or Loons – that my friend and I caught sight of on Iceland's lakes. One evening, standing on the shore of a particularly pretty stretch of water, we saw two in the distance as the May light finally began to fade, and the bird's mysterious song reached us over the ripples. These are special birds, graceful in the water, though cumbersome on land where walking is challenging on account of their legs being so far back on their bodies.

opposite: Common Eider, Iceland

above: Golden Plover, Iceland

right: Harlequin Duck, Iceland

GREYLAG GOOSE (76-89cm)

These can be captivating birds when the sunlight breathes colour into their velvety plumage. Their orange and pink beaks and sturdy pink legs frame what might otherwise be a rather dull goose from a distance. I've photographed one in minute detail on a London pond as it preened its overlapping feathers in a gentle afternoon light, and another doing some gardening among the dandelions of the Oxfordshire countryside. Look closely and there is unforeseen elegance in the architecture of the neck and wings. Remember that there is beauty on all our doorsteps, and a wintry walk to the local park can transport you into a magical realm if you stop to observe the many stories nature is telling us. Meanwhile, the Greylag Goose is not to be confused with the Pink-footed Geese I saw gathered together in an Icelandic field and which winter in their hundreds of thousands on British soil.

opposite: Greylag Goose, Kensington Gardens, London

below: Greylag Goose, Oxfordshire

CANADA GOOSE (90-110cm)

Canada Geese used to poo on our playing fields when I was at prep school in Barnes on the banks of the Thames. Rumour had it that my first headmaster took aim at the birds with a shotgun. They certainly caused a mess. Introduced from America, Canada Geese are a common sight in London and have spread across much of the country. They aren't, on first appearances, the most attractive species, but zoom in and pay attention to their black and white faces, and there is much to please the eye. This is where a photographer can help to open people's eyes to what we so often take for granted in our surroundings. Look out and up for Canada Geese flying in arrowhead formations, and flocks that can turn out to be mixed with Greylag Geese.

above: Canada Goose, Kensington Gardens, London

right: Purple Heron, Cape Town, South Africa

PURPLE HERON (78-97cm)

As a boy I longed to see a Purple Heron. Maybe because, as an unusual visitor to British shores, it was the rarer of the two herons that appeared in my miniature Collins guide book. Or maybe because, despite largely being dark grey and orange in appearance, it is described as purple in its name and therefore sounded exotic. Whatever, I was never lucky enough to glimpse one in Britain. And I would have had to be very fortunate because it is not only a rare visitor here, it is also said to be a secretive bird that can be difficult to spot. It wasn't until 2010 at the RSPB's Dungeness Nature Reserve in Kent that Purple Herons are thought to have bred successfully for the first time in the UK.

Imagine, then, the buzz when I caught sight of one flying low over wetlands on the outskirts of Cape Town. I'd made the journey alone from our hotel in Newlands through the townships that lined the road and out to the city's sewage works. Yes, you read that correctly. Of all the places I've been birdwatching, this was, on paper at least, the most surreal. But when I arrived at Strandfontein, instead of a toxic smell, I was greeted by a bird paradise. I must have spotted more than thirty species, including **Black-winged Stilts (33-36cm)**. I'd first met these delicate

black and white birds with their long thin beaks and long pink-red legs in Nairobi National Park. They'd been close to the top of my wish list after noticing them, along with a blurry African Fish Eagle, on the Instagram account of my wife's uncle who had recently visited the same reserve. But my pictures then had been unsatisfactory. Here in Strandfontein, the sleek, thick water offered a photogenic contrast to the neat outline of the stilts and I photographed three standing in a receding row in the shallows.

I also saw more than one flamboyance of **Greater Flamingos (110-150cm)**. I'd seen these bright pink birds before, too, after a long drive across Sardinia, but now I was close enough to take good photographs of them. Apparently they disturb mud with their feet, suck water through their bills and filter out algae, seeds, small shrimp, mollusks, and microscopic organisms – all of which contribute to their diet. If you wait for a Greater Flamingo to become airborne, you'll notice the rich, raw pink of its upper wing that is edged with black. This is a peculiar looking, though spectacular, species, and I caught one with my lens flying low like a slightly cumbersome, colourful arrow.

Marvellous though flamingos are, however, when I realised I'd photographed a Purple Heron in flight, the long morning walk through the South African heat became a very special one indeed. The purple hue of its wings and shoulders framed the orange of its neck and the orange-yellow bill was caught in the sunshine. Not just a highlight of the trip but of the year, and another species to add to my list of herons. I'd photographed an airborne **Western Reef Heron (55-65cm)** above a rocky beach in Zanzibar, with its pink nose and golden feet, and failed to take a sharp image of a Black-crowned Night Heron on the same island. Just days after snapping the Purple Heron, I was pointing my camera at a sunlit Black-headed Heron that was standing on top of an arch in the hotel in the Western Cape where my brother got married. Not as distinctive looking as the Western Reef Heron, the Black-headed Heron can, we're told, mix its diet of fish and frogs with large insects, birds and small mammals and doesn't rely exclusively on water to feed.

opposite: Black-winged Stilts,
Cape Town, South Africa

below: Western Reef Heron,
Zanzibar, Tanzania

overleaf: Greater Flamingo,
Cape Town, South Africa

GREY HERON (90-98cm)

Living in a land without storks that also boasts very few cranes, the Grey Heron is a long-necked prince among British birds. Its black and white beard can lend it the appearance of a wise old man as it stares intently at a pool or river, in search of fish. Herons can turn up in tiny urban gardens or be spotted looking for rodents in stubbly fields after a farmer has harvested the crop. You might have spied one loping with its deliberate wingbeat above the chimney tops of a large city, or found one on the edge of a rural riverbank as it waited patiently for a fish to reveal itself.

I must have seen hundreds of Grey Herons in my life, but one encounter on a wintry afternoon in Richmond Park stands out. It was as though two birds instead of one stood before me in the cold, dying light. One moment, the heron was hunched and dishevelled, its head feathers standing on end in the shape of a rough-hewn crown, as if fed up with the prospect of the commute home; the next, it was upright and elegant, its plumage neat and streamlined, an attractive mix of greys, black, and white. There was none of the excitement of seeing a bird for the first time, but it was thrilling to observe and capture this unexpected transformation as my subject preened itself at dusk.

More recently, I noticed a heron fishing on the edge of a neighbouring pond in the same park. Usually herons are shy and won't stand a close approach. This bird, though, seemed oblivious to my attentions, as it prepared to snatch one unsuspecting fish after another from the water. I photographed the activity in minute detail as its dangerous beak pierced another victim and a drop of blood dripped back towards the surface. Both the eye of the bird and of the fish were in sharp focus. I've chosen the image opposite, however, on account of the light that plays on the triumvirate of bird, fish and water.

opposite, overleaf left and right:
Grey Heron, Richmond Park, London

COMMON CRANE (110-120cm)

Who wouldn't want to a see a Crane for the first time? On a hot summer's day I drove from London to Slimbridge Wetland Centre in Gloucestershire. I'd heard that wild Cranes had made their nest there and that a chick or two had recently hatched. The centre's main attractions are the captive birds it keeps, but the Cranes were nesting on a tiny island just off a stretch of marshland and in full view of one of the hides. By the time I arrived, other enthusiasts with long lenses or binoculars were already in position. And there it was, a stunning bird adorned mostly in shades of grey but with a prominent white ear patch, a red eye and lovely red headspot shimmering in the English sun. I photographed the enormous specimen with its long, elegant neck protruding from the daisies that were leaning up towards the light. The real excitement, though, took hold when two golden babies, only a few days old (if that), emerged from the long grass to the water's edge. In one of my pictures, an adult is stretching down to feed a chick tenderly with something very muddy. Tasty I'm sure, if you're a tiny Crane.

Noticeably larger than the Grey Heron and much heavier and bulkier in body, Cranes are omnivorous and I photographed one of the Somerset birds with a slimy rodent in its powerful beak. That I was able to see these incredible birds was thanks to The Great Crane Project, an initiative which returned the iconic creatures to the southwest of England between 2010 and 2014. Eggs were collected in Germany before hatching here and ninety-three Common Cranes were hand-reared for release onto the Somerset Levels and Moors. The British Crane population has doubled as a consequence. A combination of hunting (what extraordinary vandalism!) and the draining of wetlands had led to the once widespread species becoming extinct in the UK before the birds underwent a natural revival in the late 1970s. A British chick fledged for the first time in four centuries on the Norfolk Broads in 1982 and Cranes now also breed regularly, though in fragile numbers, in Cambridgeshire, Suffolk, Yorkshire and North East Scotland.

The Great Crane Project is a success story to be trumpeted far and wide. It is a sign of a civilised society when our wildlife is nurtured and protected with such spectacular results for us all to enjoy.

Common Crane, Gloucestershire

MUTE SWAN (140-160cm)

Is there a more graceful bird? Study the neck of a Mute Swan as it bends above the water, wait for a pair to form heart shapes beak to beak, or just admire the reflected form of a single bird shimmering in the water. Everyday beauty at its finest. But these aren't just elegant creatures, they can be fierce, too, and will ward off threats to their nests and young with a frightening hissing noise followed, if required, by a physical assault. Still, despite their substantial size, Mute Swans are primarily, to my eye at least, birds of peaceful revery as they float apparently effortlessly along waterways through town and country.

I've watched them closely on the Round Pond in Kensington Gardens, marvelled at their grandeur on rural wetlands, and photographed a mother warming her eggs on a large nest on the banks of a pond in Hampstead Heath. An orange and black bill clearly distinguishes the Mute Swan from the much rarer – in Britain anyway – Bewick's and Whooper species, whose beaks are yellow and black. I photographed what I thought, until writing this profile, was a Bewick's Swan on an Icelandic lake. Paying closer attention, now, to subtle differences in the bill, I realise that what I captured was in fact the larger **Whooper Swan (140-160cm)**.

opposite: Mute Swan with cygnets, Somerset

below: Mute Swan with eggs, Hampstead Heath, London

Mute Swan, Kensington Gardens, London

Whooper Swan, Iceland

Visitors

One of the great excitements for the birdwatcher is a new arrival. Each spring and autumn, birds flock to our shores from far away lands. Warblers, Swallows, Sand and House Martins arrive between March and May. In September and October migrant birds reach our coastlines to feed in great numbers along the winter wetlands and mudflats that help frame the British Isles.

Among our more regular visitors, rarities also make it here each year. Few seem to do so without catching the keen eye of a twitcher or inquisitive local, and as news spreads, birders from up and down the land will themselves flock to the shrub or cliff where an unexpected migrant has briefly made its home. Millions of miles are travelled each year as twitchers pursue their passion with a fervour that bemuses the casual bystander.

In recent years I've crossed countless counties in search of vagrants and spent hours on wetlands humming with visiting water birds. From sightings of the marvellous Glossy Ibis on the Somerset Levels, to the Bearded Tits feeding in London's Hyde Park, I've rarely been disappointed when I've set off in search of a particular species.

From a photographer's perspective, it doesn't get much better than the February afternoon I spent with a quartet of Waxwings on an Oxford street. I was able to get close enough to shoot the birds feeding on plump red berries and eventually, overcoming the challenges of the bright afternoon light, managed to avoid merely a collection of silhouettes.

Cuckoo, Thursley Common, Surrey

NIGHTINGALE (15-16.5cm)

When I wrote an article for *The Telegraph* about my love of birdwatching in 2015, I sent it to the uncle who had helped ignite my interest in birds, back in the late eighties. He enjoyed the piece but pointed out that I'd made no mention of song – which to him had "always been half the joy of bird observation". He was absolutely right: I had been ignoring my ears and relying entirely on my eyes for decades. In the years since, however, I have listened ever more intently to the sometimes subtle, often definitive differences between the birds that I'm hoping to see.

There is, as my uncle encouraged me to discover, great pleasure to be taken in listening out for the call from the canopy, the hail from the hedgerow. Not only are the melodies rich and varied, the notes help to alert us to the presence of a particular species and to differentiate between those which otherwise might be almost indistinguishable. Take the Willow Warbler. Even to the trained eye it is nearly identical to the Chiffchaff – at least without forensic examination! Yet it is relatively straightforward to tell its charming tune apart from the Chiffchaff's relentless chiffchaffing.

In contrast to the familiar, though camera shy, sweet-singing Blackbird, the Nightingale is an elusive summer visitor, and it wasn't until 2016 that I could first be sure I'd heard the bird made famous in Keats' poem. Listening to its translucent, varied notes is a haunting experience and high up on the priority list of bird and nature lovers alike.

If Keats was moved by the Nightingale's notes, then so can we all be. As he wrote in his Ode:

'Tis not through envy of thy happy lot,
But being too happy in thine happiness,—
That thou, light-winged Dryad of the trees
In some melodious plot
Of beechen green, and shadows numberless,
Singest of summer in full-throated ease.

I'd listened to my mother's stories of Nightingales singing in her childhood. Once, maybe, I'd heard the bird myself calling from the foliage of a French garden in the Valley of the Lot. Not, though, until I had rediscovered my love of birds, did I set out on a journey to see and photograph this rather drab, almost ungainly, songbird.

The RSPB reserve at Pulborough is a gem, tucked away in the East Sussex countryside. Like so many of our conservation areas, water plays an important role in the reserve's success, but its fields and hedgerows are also host to a variety of species. Depending on the season, you might see Lesser Whitethroat, Greenfinch, Sparrowhawk, Short-eared Owl, and Peregrine Falcon as well as the birds that feed on the wetlands themselves. On a hot spring or summer day you'll find adders enjoying the sunshine in Adder Alley, too.

I'd hoped to see a Hen Harrier when I first visited the site, but I'd have been lucky. Instead, I returned in search of the Nightingale. I have once or twice confused the notes of the Song Thrush with those of our most famous songster, but to the initiated, the two birds are easy enough to tell apart. The Nightingale's song is otherworldly and stirs imaginings of distant times with its sometimes sweet, sometimes harsh trills.

Other birdwatchers had arrived with similar intent, and little clusters dotted Adder's Alley as I approached with my camera. And then there it was, perched midway up a tree, unexpectedly unspectacular in its plumage. I struggled with my lens to capture it sharply between the leaves but a little later the bird – or perhaps a relative – re-emerged in the undergrowth and hunted for worms just metres from me in the shade. This was a time before I invested in a more powerful lens so I will have to return one day in the hope of a better picture.

Like the Cuckoo, the Nightingale rightly holds a special place in the hearts not just of birdwatchers like me, but of all those who share an appreciation of the lyrical traditions of this country. These are birds that call to us from down the ages, and still adorn our countryside with their sounds of summer.

Later that same year, I spotted a Nightingale again, this time in boggy land on the Albanian coast, and listened to the famous "jug jug" of its now familiar voice. Except it doesn't really "jug jug" at all. Its throaty call is perhaps responsible for the phrase but even that sounds more like an angry rattle, in contrast to the fluty notes of its memorable song.

WAXWING (18cm)

Since leaving the BBC in the spring of 2013, my professional life has, to a great extent, allowed me the freedom to choose my working hours, and I'm often able to escape to a bird reserve.

Otmoor, a watery haven close to Oxford and within relatively comfortable range of West London, is, as has probably become clear by now, a favourite. I've seen Sedge and Reed Warblers at close quarters, and eyed a Cetti's as it edges along a soaking briar on a rainy summer's day. I've spotted Redshank, Lapwing and a variety of ducks enjoying the fertile land, and observed Barn and Short-eared Owl, Hobby, Marsh Harrier and Sparrowhawk. Hen Harriers have been known to visit, too, and I once caught a glimpse of a male Merlin, dressed in grey, darting low across the ground. I've photographed Golden Plover catching the sun, as they flocked in huge numbers overhead, and witnessed murmurations of Starlings darkening the evening sky during winter, as thousands upon thousands of the speckled birds prepared to roost above the marshes. But I'm almost always in a rush.

So in the winter of early 2017 I faced a choice. Continue to the boardwalk, or abandon the reserve in search of a dreamy sighting on a busy Oxford street. As I was taking pictures of the Goldfinches on the reserve's feeders, an RSPB volunteer had given me directions to a quartet of Waxwings devouring berries in front of a townhouse twenty minutes away. I had watched a community of the slightly smaller Cedar Waxwing in action in a Santa Barbara garden a year earlier, but I couldn't be sure I had ever seen our plumper species.

There was, of course, a risk that I'd arrive too late, but my mind was made up. I returned to the car and headed for the outskirts of Oxford. The tell-tale signs of a special nature event in full flow greeted me first: a huddle of men and women with cameras and binoculars trained on an innocuous tree. I was just in time because the birds had almost stripped a tree bare of its bright red berries. What a discovery! Four Waxwings, definitively crested, painted in red, yellow and peach with bold black eye masks. So emphatic is their colouring they almost seem fake.

Passersby stopped to ask what all the fuss was about. Who, but a birdwatcher, would guess at the excitement on show? And who, I wonder, first spotted these winter visitors filling their bellies with juicy fruit? I managed to take some successful shots. The ultimate goal, as you learn quickly from Instagram, is to frame the bird with a berry clasped in its beak.

During the winter months, Waxwings can apparently munch their way through roughly double their body weight in berries in a single day. When numbers outgrow the available food on their foreign breeding grounds, irruptions may flock to our shores. If we're lucky we might welcome up to twelve thousand birds in a season, though we could be visited by as few as several dozen. They tend to arrive from October and can stay until April.

While there's no predicting where Waxwings might alight, it's worth keeping a lookout on rowan and hawthorn trees, heavy with berries during the colder months, just in case. We know by now that the prettiest or rarest birds can turn up in the most inauspicious of habitats and this is true, too, of the Waxwing, which has been recorded visiting supermarket car parks, thanks to their berry-bearing ornamental shrubs. Eastern Britain as well as the east of Northern Ireland are among the areas of the UK most favoured by the species, but as evidenced by my Oxfordshire sighting, they can also travel to unexpected parts of the country in search of food.

SWALLOW (17-19cm)

A reassuring and familiar visitor. "One Swallow may not a summer make", but the warmer months wouldn't be the same without these stylish acrobats, dipping and diving on lazy afternoons and sun-soaked evenings. Down by the stream in the Welsh valley that stretches out before my parents' place, they sweep low over the lush meadow and mingle with House Martins as they hunt down insects on the wing.

Lucky you if there are Swallows nesting in your barn. We did have House Martins making homes in our eaves but they left as suddenly as they arrived and we've missed them ever since. House Martins are distinguishable from Swallows by their shorter tales, stockier frame, stubbier wings and white rumps. Swallows wear inky blue coats on their backs with a deep red handkerchief around their necks. I've watched Sand Martins – sandy-coloured cousins of

the House Martin – play along a Welsh riverbank, Swifts, larger and pointier than Swallows, dart high in the sky and even a Red-rumped Swallow arrow low over the Corsican countryside, but none are quite as elegant as the silky Swallow. They lend a lyricism to our landscapes before they depart again at summer's end.

Photographing Swallows on the wing can be a thankless exercise, and it's one I have failed to master. Such is their speed in flight that I'm always left with a series of blurred images. I have, though, enjoyed more luck with the birds that alight on the balcony of my wife's grandfather's Pembrokeshire cottage. Crouching down to the level of the handrail, I was able to capture them polishing their sleek coats in the wet against the bright green backdrop of the grass beyond.

previous spread: Waxwings, Oxford

left and opposite: Swallow, Pembrokeshire

CUCKOO (32-34cm)

The quintessential sound of our late spring and early summer, the Cuckoo's eponymous and unmistakable song seems to echo down the ages. As a birdwatcher, the fact that, with early adulthood already behind me, I still hadn't seen one of these iconic birds, nagged at me. During an early summer's morning at Otmoor, my mother was sure she'd seen a Cuckoo in flight while I dragged behind photographing other birds. It was a thrill for her as the Cuckoo's song was a signature music of her childhood. But I missed it. And so, more determined than ever, I returned the next morning, early enough to give myself the best chance of a sighting. Within minutes, and with the help of another birder, I finally set eyes on the blue grey shape of a male perched on a distant tree.

Although my focus these days is marginally more on bird photography than birdwatching itself, photographing birds has got me excited again about seeing species for the first time and building my life list. How, at the age of 37, could I have taken myself seriously as a birdwatcher without having seen a Cuckoo? Now that I had, at long last, set eyes upon the bird, I wanted to photograph it successfully. To that end, I met up with my doctor friend from Oxfordshire, all the way down in Somerset at the Ham Wall RSPB Reserve. Together, we spotted the Glossy Ibis, a rare visitor to Britain, and I photographed a Hobby hunting high overhead in the evening sun. A fleeting Cuckoo, though, was too quick for me and I left disappointed again.

Eventually, I learned through Instagram of a Cuckoo called 'Colin'. Yes, really. Every year, Colin migrates from Africa to a corner of the Surrey countryside where he has learned to feed in full view on the prompting of keen birdwatchers and photographers. Maggots and tiny worms are put out for him in a field and he comes to have his fill two or three times a day. His feeders, who are members of the public, even erect mossy branches for him to perch on for the benefit of the photographers. I waited in the hot June sun of 2018 for at least an hour, and despite his reputed tameness there was still an element of doubt as to whether he would reappear.

Eventually he did, announcing himself with his familiar 'cuckoo' call, and landing first on the tree above our heads before, emboldened, flying down for his lunch. I took so many crisp shots with pretty green backgrounds that I risked clogging up my laptop. His smart silver head offset the bright yellow eye and his striped chest complemented his orange feet. My images revealed a stain across his chest, too – presumably the faded blood of juicy worms.

The question is, though, was I cheating? I uploaded my best shots to social media, but the warm glow of 'mission accomplished' was tinged with a hint of hollowness. Yes, the bird was wild. No, those feeding Colin didn't seem to be doing him any harm. Yes, the spectacle has afforded many photographers the chance to take and share stunning images of a shy beauty that would otherwise be almost entirely out of the reach of our lenses. But, there was no denying the event was staged.

And then again, was this any different, in artistic terms, to taking photographs of birds on garden feeders? Maybe not. So long as one is open about how the image was acquired. In recent months I've been shocked and disappointed to learn that many of the pictures on Instagram of Sparrowhawks and, in Holland, of Goshawks (a bird I still long to see) are also staged. Private hides charge for photographers to spend the day waiting for and then snapping these mighty birds of prey as they feed off small birds left out for them. The prey might even be pinned to a post, I've been told, in order that the raptor stays to eat its meal in plain sight of the cameras. I've engaged in a debate about the practice with the owner of a British Sparrowhawk hide, and he argues that he takes daily care of the birds' interests and is dedicated to their wellbeing. Ultimately, however, I think that a photograph does lose something of its magic when you know it's been set up. Still, I've included my Cuckoo pictures in this book so you can decide for yourself and, as you'll discover in the Owls section, I even paid money myself to photograph a Little Owl in Buckinghamshire.

above and previous page: Cuckoo,
Thursley Common, Surrey

Cuckoos are, to my eye, spectacular birds, although to some they may appear little more exciting to look at than a pigeon. In flight they can resemble a Sparrowhawk and they have the air of a raptor about them. They arrive in late April and early May, and the female lays her eggs in the nests of other species – such as Meadow Pipits, Dunnocks and Reed Warbler – when they're not looking, and after having removed one of the host's eggs first. Some cheek! There is a remarkable picture on Instagram of a Reed Warbler feeding a comparatively giant baby Cuckoo. Since adults play no part in rearing their young, they tend to leave our shores again in July and are among the first of our summer visitors to depart. Once fully fledged, juvenile birds follow them around a month later.

Sadly, Cuckoos have declined significantly in number in Britain and much of the countryside has been stripped of its plaintive refrain. I will always thrill to the call of the Cuckoo and be mindful that they are a remarkable species. What a feat it is that young birds can migrate thousands of miles without ever having been introduced to their parents! When I saw an African Cuckoo , similar in appearance to our own, I had flown thousands of miles myself – but with the help of British Airways. We were on safari in the Masai Mara and I photographed the bird in the Kenyan rain. Just as excitingly, a Red-breasted Cuckoo played catch-me-if-you-can with my camera yards from our tent, just out of range of a true shot. Had it not been for the threat of wild, meat-eating animals, I would have followed it further into the bush!

Foreign Birds

I f one of the delights of birdwatching is its accessibility – you can as we've seen, enjoy birdlife from the comfort of your home – then another is certainly its transportability. Wherever you are in the world, there will always be birds – and often unfamiliar and thrilling species. My ornithological preoccupations make every foreign trip that bit more enjoyable, and exciting.

In the days before I owned my first mobile phone, identification proved more challenging, and I probably missed as many as 300 species on my travels. These days, though, I'm almost never offline and that means I'm nearly always able to identify the birds that I photograph.

While the subtle beauty of our own British birds is beyond dispute, it's equally true that some of the species on view in countries as far flung as India and Australia (where Sulphur-crested Cockatoos once appeared on a friend's balcony) are more exotic in their colouring and sometimes more arresting in their shape and size, too. I've been lucky in the extent of my travels and have seen more than two thirds of the birds on my six hundred-strong life list overseas. Holidays are now planned with one eye on the local birdlife, and even my honeymoon included many hours of birdwatching!

And why not? I've stood on the shores of a remote lake in southern Iceland and heard the haunting call of the Great Northern Diver; I've watched Short-toed Snake Eagles hunt in Italy and France, and I've shared a Caribbean morning view with a Little Blue Heron in Saint Lucia. I can compare from memory the rival colours of the Little Bee-eater and the Green Bee-eater; I've been close to both the European Roller in the south of France and its Lilac-breasted relative in South Africa, Kenya and Tanzania, and I've marvelled at hummingbirds and the speed of their wingbeat in North America.

From the lupine hillsides of Tuscany to the jungles of Maharashtra, from the vineyards of Provence to an international cricket stadium in Lahore, and from Cape Town's gardens to the otherworldly landscapes south-east of Reykjavik, the world is a wonderful place for the birdwatcher.

Orange-breasted Sunbird,
Kirstenbosch Botanical Gardens,
Cape Town, South Africa

ZITTING CISTICOLA (10-12cm)

Travelling to Malta in the hope of seeing and photographing birds probably wasn't the most educated decision I've made, given that the Maltese have shot so many of them. As I walked the cliff-tops and inland slopes, shotgun cartridges lay strewn on the ground. If an online blog is to be believed, Barn Owls and Peregrines used to hunt around the cliffs at Ta' Cenc, close to where I stayed, before they were themselves hunted to extinction. Imagine being the sort of person who would take aim at one of these precious species – or indeed at any wild bird. And Malta is in the EU! Tragically, there is a subculture of shooting wild birds in parts of the Mediterranean and, astonishingly, it is still lawful to shoot Woodcock (as well as other species) in the UK, despite our native Woodcock population being said to be in decline. I support a total ban on hunting wild birds in Britain, although it is true that some wetland areas, preserved for the hunting of wildfowl, do also play a role in conservation.

Predictably, I would leave the islands of Gozo and Malta with only a single photographic contender for this book: a delightful, though far from rare, Zitting Cisticola – and if you think that's an eccentric name, you obviously haven't heard of the Bearded Tit. I first came across this common Cisticola in the rugged hills of Tuscany that sloped down from our hotel opposite the town of Montepulciano, but I spent a great deal of effort in searing temperatures trying to photograph the species in the Maltese early Autumn.

Notwithstanding my unwarranted disappointment at failing to return home with a file full of pictures from a three-and-a-half day solo trip to the Mediterranean, I did have the unexpected joy of discovering birds I had never seen before while going through my ID photos on my final night. The warblers I had assumed to be exclusively the colourful but common Sardinian Warbler (which I'd already seen in Sardinia two summers previously) also seemed to include not only the Subalpine Warbler (huge excitement!) but even the Spectacled Warbler! Such a boon, and worth the tens of thousands of steps I'd walked in the draining heat with my camera. The intensity of this joy, however, was short-lived and matched only by the later dejection when – on even closer inspection – I had to accept that what I'd thought was a female Subalpine Warbler was in fact a Sardinian Warbler all along. Still, the Spectacled Warbler, together with the Spanish Sparrow and Blue Rock Thrush, Malta's national bird, added up to three new species for the trip. By no means a disaster.

There were, though, further moments of disappointment on my Maltese adventure. After taking the ferry back to the mainland to visit one of the islands' bird reserves, I found it closed for the summer. I did, however, take the opportunity to return to the wooded area known as Buskett Woods that I'd visited on my first afternoon, on the grounds that it is said to be a superb spot for watching migrating raptors towards the end of September. I may have been a few days too early, but I noticed suddenly that the high heavens were populated by four or five circling Honey Buzzards.

I was also led on my usual merry dance by the frustratingly evasive European Bee-eaters and heard but couldn't lay eyes on a Red-backed Shrike. I don't suppose, despite the stunning coastal sunsets, I'll be returning to the islands with my camera any time soon.

Orange-breasted Sunbird,
Kirstenbosch Botanical Gardens,
Cape Town, South Africa

SOUTHERN DOUBLE-COLLARED SUNBIRD (12cm)

The Kirstenbosch Botanical Gardens nestle in the bosom of Table Mountain in one of the leafier suburbs of Cape Town. On a clear day, the views extend across to the waterfront and to the Atlantic Ocean. Even if you're not a bird enthusiast, you can't fail to see the beauty on display: an already spectacular location is bejewelled by flowerbeds flaming in reds, oranges and yellows. But for the bird photographer, the gardens are an even rarer treat, offering as they do stunning backdrops to some of South Africa's most eye-catching pollen-feeders.

As I walked between the flowerbeds in the February heat, **Cape Sugarbirds (34-44cm)**, endemic to the Cape, perched on trees or clambered on sturdy flowers to access nectar with their long, sharp beaks and long, brush-tipped tongues. The male Sugarbirds have instantly recognisable tails that are comfortably longer than their bodies and that fan out at their tips. A territorial Cape Batis peered out at my lens from the long grass bordering one of the walkways and showed off its intricately patterned feathers; a Cape Bulbul straddled the stem and flowerhead of a colourful plant as it betrayed its yellow underbelly while looking at me with its pink-rimmed eye, and an omnivorous **Red-winged Starling (27-30cm)** did similar, while showing off its glossy black plumage (though not its chestnut wing feathers).

Speckled Mousebirds hung out in the bushes and close to the tops of trees. I'd seen this species a month earlier in Kenya, and came across a cluster of **Red-faced Mousebirds (34cm)** a few days later in the stunning gardens of the Babylonstoren hotel grounds. Frugivorous birds, Red-faced Mousebirds are a sociable species, when they're not breeding, and feed in gangs. Although they are said to be more wary than other Mousebirds, I had no difficulty in approaching close enough for razor sharp shots of one of them tearing apart a juicy peach.

Back in the Kirstenbosch Botanical Gardens, the unspectacular but delightful African Dusky Flycatcher looked pretty against a golden, sun-soaked backdrop, as it paused in its pursuit of insects, and a yellow-browed **Forest Canary (12.5-13cm)**, not to be confused with the similar looking Brimstone (or Bully) Canary, munched juicy seeds with its strong bill in the dappled shade. Caught in a halo of sunlight, its red bill illuminated, a Common Waxbill balanced on a green reed and showed off a prominent red band running across its eye, and the delicately drawn stripes curving round its underbody and back. In another corner of the gardens, I hoped desperately for its cousin, the miniature **Swee Waxbill (9-10cm)**, to show me both its startling red rump and red lower mandible at the same time. Eventually I happened upon a party of three of these dainty birds performing gymnastics on strands of long grass that bent but did not entirely give way under their weight. In one of my photographs it appears as if one of the birds is asking another for a bite of the tiny meal it carries in its beak.

To my huge disappointment and enduring frustration, however, I narrowly missed a sighting of what would have been my first Malachite Sunbird. A local couple had just watched a pair fly off as I approached. You'd be unlucky, though, in these gorgeous gardens not to see an almost equally arresting relative, the Southern Double-collared Sunbird. The challenge I set myself was to photograph this multi-coloured nectar specialist with the sun on its chainmail feathers and, ideally, as it fed on a vibrant flower. I was in Cape Town for my brother's wedding and persuaded my wife to let me visit the gardens three times in one week. By the end of the trip, I had what I wanted. But not without having to discard scores of unsuccessful images. Too dark! Out of focus! Partially obscured!

Southern Double-collared Sunbird,
Kirstenbosch Botanical Gardens,
Cape Town, South Africa

left: Red-winged Starling,
Kirstenbosch Botanical Gardens,
Cape Town, South Africa

opposite: Cape Sugarbird,
Kirstenbosch Botanical Gardens,
Cape Town, South Africa

Sunbirds rarely seem to sit still. Just as you think you've framed the perfect shot, the bird finds another flower on which to feed. Patience and persistence are essential. If you get it right, the floral settings can contribute to spectacular compositions.

The most advanced bird photographers on Instagram tend to have a recognisable style. John, or @djmr3bb, is one whose work I particularly admire. He's a doctor by profession and a highly skilled amateur bird photographer in his free time. We became friends when we joined the Instragram dots while out birdwatching in Oxfordshire. There's a lyrical quality to his images and he resists the temptation to fill the screen with the bird. Instead, he likes to show his subjects in their context and his work is instantly familiar.

I tend to opt instead for closer-up images of a bird and highlight, I hope, the intricate subtlety of its appearance. I'm really asking my audience – such as it is – to admire the detail of the patterns, shape and colours. Each to his or her own, of course. But with the Cape Town sunbirds, I was happy to compromise, because the rich hues of the flowers on which they were feeding helped create such vivid profiles.

below: Forest Canary, Kirstenbosch Botanical Gardens, Cape Town, South Africa

opposite: Red-faced Mousebird, Western Cape, South Africa

overleaf: Swee Waxbills, Kirstenbosch Botanical Gardens, Cape Town, South Africa

ORANGE-BREASTED SUNBIRD (12.5-16.5cm)

Yet more spectacular than the Southern Double-collared is the Orange-breasted Sunbird. In good light, this is one of the most beautiful birds I have ever photographed. It could, quite reasonably, be called the Rainbow-coloured Sunbird. The head is a riot of rich blues, violets and greens that make way for deep oranges, and then yellows as chest becomes underbelly. I must have taken more than a hundred images as I tried to capture the species with the sun catching its unmistakable and eponymous breast.

A photographer's dream, Orange-breasted Sunbirds are endemic to southwestern South Africa so you have to travel to see them. I caught sight of my first, high up on a tree in our Cape Town hotel garden. Once you've noticed its tummy you know you're in the presence of something special – but they almost danced with me in the Kirstenbosch Botanical Gardens, teasing me as they flitted from flower to flower. The curved bill is typical of the sunbird family and while it does take insects – often in flight – it seems to focus its feeding on nectar.

There is an anatomical caveat with sunbirds. Those who find the creatures of the avian world scary are unlikely to appreciate the long claw-like, black toes. Even I find them just a little eery in pictures! That said, the feet have an obvious function as they allow the birds to cling, like colourful acrobats, sideways and sometimes upside down, to the tendrils of the plants they feed on.

Orange-breasted Sunbird,
Kirstenbosch Botanical Gardens,
Cape Town, South Africa

LITTLE BEE-EATER (15-17cm)

The Olare Motorogi Conservancy in Kenya's Masai Mara was the setting for the first few days of my honeymoon. It's a special place that teems with animal and birdlife. Within fifty metres or so of watching hippos lazing in a muddy river, we caught sight of a gorgeous little bird. Perched squat against a gnarled branch was the Little Bee-eater. As with Kingfishers, adding a species to my list of Bee-eaters is skin-tinglingly happy-making. I still can't quite explain why it feels so special to know that I've spotted a particular bird. No one else in the world cares what I've seen with my own eyes. Only I do. (Unless you count the vicarious excitement my wife and mother experience on my behalf). There's just something intoxicating about spotting a beautiful bird for the first time.

The Little Bee-eater is so exquisite, partly because it is an unusual variation on a theme. You can tell it's a bee-eater by the curve of the beak, by the eye and by the shape of the head, but it is in miniature form. I don't normally recognise the word when casual enthusiasts describe birds as 'sweet'. However, just as the African Pygmy Kingfisher is undeniably 'cute', so too is the Little Bee-eater. And it's very lovely to look at too. The head feathers are mottled blue, green and brown; its eye is ruby-red; it boasts a jet black eye-stripe and bright yellow chin and its black necklace, which matches the eye-stripe, bleeds out into burnt orange. I love it.

The bird I saw, typically for the species, was sitting on a perch low to the ground from where it would no doubt sally forth to capture insects, particularly bees, wasps and hornets, mid-flight. Keep an eye out for these tiny bundles of colour near to sandy banks and aardvarks' holes, where they make their nests.

Little Bee-eater,
Masai Mara, Kenya

STRIPED KINGFISHER (16-18cm)

I have a thing about Kingfishers. It has grown from the magic of our own species, a tiny orange-tinted sapphire as it flashes up and downstream. But it also has something to do with the size of the beak and shape of the head, features common to others in the family. In Tanzania I saw a Pied Kingfisher on the island of Zanzibar, and in Kenya I found four members of the clan: the Striped, Grey-headed, African Pygmy and Malachite. I discovered the Striped Kingfisher sitting, implausibly, on a tree punctuated by savage thorns as we headed out on an evening game drive during our honeymoon safari. Not all Kingfishers actually fish, and this bird feeds largely on grasshoppers, occasionally also taking little lizards, snakes and rodents. It is said to guard its territory fiercely and drives off other birds of the same species, as well as shrikes, rollers and doves. Look at the bird in my photograph and it's impossible not to be impressed by its poise as it ignores the deadly-looking thorns that surround it.

Slightly larger is the **Grey-headed Kingfisher (21cm)**. I photographed this species perched on a thick branch that matched its grey-brown head. The beak is a bright red-orange that finds a paler echo in its tummy. A patient hunter of insects and small lizards as it sits still for extended periods, this is a sumptuous species with an electric blue tail and fringe to its wing feathers.

The **African Pygmy Kingfisher (12cm)** is the tiniest species we came across and we spied it sitting above a river, although, like its Striped and Grey-headed relatives, it doesn't fish but feeds on a varied diet that includes insects, lizards, frogs, and the occasional crab. Its minute size made it difficult to photograph from a distance, and I ended up with a blur of violet, blue and orange feathers and a splash of red belonging to the protruding red beak. The eye-catching **Malachite Kingfisher (13cm)** is only a centimetre larger than the Pygmy, and we encountered this miniature fisherman low above a river we were crossing in our safari truck. Despite the expert driving of our guide Charles, who was attentive to my every twitch, I was unable to free the bird in my frame from distracting foliage. Eventually I did manage to capture the kingfisher without the bright green leaves of a tree actually obstructing its body or beak but I would have loved to have had a clean background. The Malachite is similar looking to our Kingfisher but the blue of its back is brushed with indigo.

top: Grey-headed Kingfisher
middle: African Pygmy Kingfisher
bottom: Malachite Kingfisher,
all Masai Mara, Kenya

opposite: Striped Kingfisher,
Masai Mara, Kenya

GREEN BEE-EATER (16-18cm)

Daniel was the resident birdwatcher and nature guide at The Machan in the Indian jungle. A hotel consisting of a series of tree houses two and a half hours from the busy streets of Mumbai, one of its attractions is the birdlife in and around the canopies. Within three days I added almost forty species to my list, inside and outside the grounds. Without Daniel's help, however, I would have struggled to achieve half that bird count, and it is a joy, even for an experienced birdwatcher, to spend time in the company of an expert. Still in his early twenties, Daniel had already travelled the world, working on conservation projects, and here he was leading tours of guests.

Some of those who joined Daniel's tour of the forest were, like me, genuine enthusiasts; others uninitiated but interested. On my penultimate afternoon we set out on a trek, just the two of us, under hot, clear blue skies. I'd seen European Bee-eaters in all their technicolor during summer stays in Tuscany, but Daniel only just stopped short of promising me that we'd come face to face with Green Bee-eaters on our walk. After half an hour, though, not a single one.

The views were spectacular as we kept an eye out for snakes and passed lazy, long-horned cows sheltering from the sun. Locals in brightly coloured clothes carried water jars on their heads and zipped past on crowded trucks or riding motorcycles. A female cowherd lent on her stick.

There are never any guarantees as a birdwatcher, and I've endured many frustrating outings. But then, suddenly, your luck can change. We spotted the bottle green of two bee-eaters high in a tree. As is so often the case once you've seen a bird for the first time, a second sighting soon materialised. Not only that, the next day my driver, charged with returning me to the magnificence and pollution of Mumbai, first indulged Daniel and me as we took the road east, deeper into the outback. Soon, birds perched plentifully on telegraph wires, some with insects trapped in their beaks, and posed just long enough for the photographer.

Sadly, the results of my efforts were disappointing as I struggled to do justice to the Green Bee-eaters in silhouette. I failed to capture properly their orange crowns that are met by black eye-stripes, which themselves are underscored by a turquoise fringe. Different greens compete for prominence amid the back feathers and underbelly plumage and, sitting on a branch overhanging a creek, a member of this lovely species resembled a jewel studding its rural backdrop. In a country crammed full of almost every conceivable colour, these birds still managed to stand out in their luminous feathers.

EUROPEAN BEE-EATER (27-29cm)

For three summers out of four we stayed in a rustic hotel in the Italian hills opposite the medieval magnificence of Montepulciano and within a short drive of pretty Piensa. Hotel Lupaia is a rare find in an idyllic setting and takes its name from the wolves that are said to live in the valley. We've watched baby boar feed in the early twilight during an evening drive, eaten truffle pasta as the sun dipped behind a distant church tower, and visited one of the vineyards that fills our bottles with Montepulciano wine.

Sitting by the pool one afternoon, I noticed a commotion in the air above us. The piping calls of a busy European Bee-eater colony! You'd be incredibly fortunate to bump into a single bird in Britain – they're a very rare vagrant – so these were my first. With its chestnut head, turquoise chest and buttercup-yellow neck, the Bee-eater is an obviously stunning bird. But, while they can perch within tantalisingly close range and while at least once – and in snake country – I took my trainers off to creep closer, they almost always jump off in a hurry, just as I'm about to steady myself for the longed-for shot. I've had much more luck with other bee-eater species around the world, although on the last morning of our most recent trip to Italy, after we'd stopped the car en route to Pisa airport, a bird sat still long enough for me to photograph it in the morning light. Despite hours of stalking treetops and telephone wires in the French heat of the Luberon, I haven't yet bettered the shot.

BLUE-CHEEKED BEE-EATER (31cm)

No snakes, no snakes! Two Zanzibaris were trying to convince me in broken English that there really were no snakes around, as we waded knee-deep through the tropical brush in search of exotic birds. I was once told that Sardinia was devoid of poisonous snakes so maybe, I tried to convince myself, the same was true of the island of Zanzibar off the Tanzanian coast. It wasn't. Later in this second leg of our honeymoon, the man who guided me through the Jacani forest in search of the red colobus monkeys revealed that when birds suddenly stir in the tree, it might very well be on account of a green mamba writhing its way from branch to branch. There are, it turned out, various species of deadly snake in Zanzibar. Sufficiently reassured by my local companions, however, I plunged on towards a flash of gold that belonged, I discovered, to an African Golden Oriole. Soon we found a Blue-cheeked Bee-eater, too, pausing invitingly but in silhouette on a tree.

Only later in the week, when I took a boat out to the mangroves, would I have the chance to photograph this well-dressed bird in a way that honoured its rich plumage. Things, though, got off to an inauspicious start. The water was too low for our punt to penetrate the mangroves themselves and I spent more than an uncomfortable moment wondering whether we might run aground and become stranded. The taxi driver who had delivered me to the drop-off point for what was advertised as a birdwatching experience had also joined us aboard and was even more nervous than me because he couldn't swim.

Having failed at first to see anything but a Cattle Egret on a watery trip that had promised so much, at last I spotted what seemed to be a Little Bittern. What excitement! The smaller version of our more familiar Bittern would have been worth the stress and anxiety of the expedition all on its own. When it turned out, in fact, to be a Striated Heron, I was almost as thrilled. And then I spotted the Blue-cheeked Bee-eater again, resting or preparing perhaps to dive for an unsuspecting bee and framed by jungly foliage. Even from the unsteadiness of the boat, I took strong photographs of these sleek birds against lime-green backgrounds that complemented the bottle greens of their feathers. With its ruby eye set in a black stripe that divides the turquoise eyebrow from a turquoise cheek; the rusty neck below a yellow chin; the slim aerodynamic body and elegant, slender beak, this is a species to hold its own among the prettiest in East Africa.

EUROPEAN ROLLER (29-32cm)

As the bird flew out across the vines from above my head, I knew immediately it was something 'special'. Its broad wings, indented with electric blue, indicated exoticism and, likely, scarcity. Fortuitously, this shape that was now the object of my absolute attention, alighted on a tree that fringed the vineyard. I was birdwatching in the midst of a quintessentially Provençal scene. My long lens is a greater aid than any binoculars and, more often than not, I can rely on it to

help me with identification after even the briefest of encounters.

With a 500mm zoom you can pick out birds from improbable distances, although summer foliage often gets in the way of a sharp image. I crept closer, picking my way through the hot, sun-drenched vines and, so infused was I with the thrill of my mission, I was almost tempted to remove my shoes. But the advantages of a silent approach were offset by the threat of vipers. I had at least chosen my route carefully and wound my way behind the screening of the tree in the hope of reaching my target undetected. No luck. It had flown. Of course.

Still, I had my distant shots to examine and they revealed a bird that did indeed prove unfamiliar. A Roller. My excitement, though, was at first tinged with the indignity of unjustified disappointment. Twenty years earlier I had seen a Lilac-breasted Roller on a South African game reserve and so this, while an unexpected pleasure, appeared not to be a 'lifer' – the term birders use to describe a species they have spotted for the first time.

Yet comparing the bird in my frame with its lilac cousin yielded uncertain results. There was too much blue and less variation in the plumage. What joy, then, to discover seconds later that Lilac-breasted Rollers are birds exclusive to Africa and are not found in France. This was my first European Roller!

And, just as wonderfully, the adrenalin of the search had drawn me into an Elysian dream. Poppies sprung up among the daisies that lifted their faces to the sky between the olive trees. Other birds were singing, too, and I abandoned hopes of taking a superior shot of the Roller, charmed as I was by the call of Serins from the neighbouring pines. A raptor, probably a Black Kite, circled high overhead, a darkened speck in the deep midday blue.

There was activity, too, back at the house where I had parked my car on the edge of the vines. A van had disgorged its occupants for what appeared to be a lunch party. As I made my way back, the Roller reappeared, clinging now to one of the thick telegraph wires that can line the fields of the Luberon. Almost silently, I moved tantalisingly close, but alerted just too soon to my ambitions, it flew once again and I was forced to make do with adding this colourful species to my life list.

A crow-sized bird, the European Roller eats beetles, locusts, flies and other invertebrates but can also take frogs, lizards, snakes, and even small birds. Thanks to its hunting technique, it can afford good views as it perches prominently in search of food. And, if you find yourself in Tanzania in April, you might catch its crowded coastal flight as it migrates north. Rollers travel thousands of miles each spring and autumn between their European and Asian breeding areas and sub-Saharan Africa. Once safely arrived at their northern destinations, each pair will defend a territory and build a family of baby Rollers.

Finally, I rounded the foliage at the corner of the field and the little group I'd noticed from afar revealed themselves not to be picnickers after all, but French birdwatchers! Their lenses were trained on a distant tree. Did they know something I did not? Had news travelled of a rare species in the area? It turned out, with the help of Google Translate, that their attention was drawn to the common Collared Dove and the chief objects of their curiosity were the local Bee-eaters. I showed them a close-up I'd managed earlier in the week and encouraged them in the direction of the European Roller. I wonder whether they found it.

Blue-cheeked Bee-eater, Zanzibar, Tanzania

AFRICAN WATTLED LAPWING (34cm)

Of the two lapwing species we saw in the Mara, the **African Wattled Lapwing (34cm)** was perhaps the more eye-catching. Its bright yellow legs match the yellow of its eye ring, black-tipped beak and facial wattle. But the **Blacksmith Lapwing (31cm)** – or Blacksmith Plover – is also striking with its black, white and grey plumage and dark red eye. Meanwhile, the much smaller Three-banded Plover, similar in size to the Ringed Plovers found in Britain,

presented itself low to the ground, close to a watering hole in the Nairobi National Park, as we were watching a lounging crocodile. Sweet-looking – the plover, not the crocodile – with an orange eye-ring and pink base to its bill, it eats insects, worms and other invertebrates. What a contrast it made to the relatively giant eagles, spoonbills and ibises – not to mention the hippos and giraffes – with whom it shared the landscape.

left: African Wattled Lapwing, Masai Mara, Kenya

opposite: Blacksmith Lapwing, Masai Mara, Kenya

LILAC-BREASTED ROLLER (36-38cm)

Our honeymoon to Kenya and Tanzania was not without its dramas. There was the deep stress of not feeling safe in our own bed in the Mara Conservancy, separated only by canvas from murderous hyenas on the outer fringe of a six tent camp plonked in the middle of lion territory. There was the pounding of my heart when I was woken from a fretful sleep by an angry roar that seemed metres from where we slept. There was my panic when we heard what I took to be hordes of marauding lions outside before being told by a guard, bearing only a small club and a dagger, that they weren't lions at all, and learning in the morning that they had in fact been about one hundred wildebeest. There was the thunder and lightning as it cracked around our makeshift home in the middle of the night and the rain that whipped its sides as the wind flapped aggressively at the fabric walls during the worst storm the camp had endured in seven years. Later, there was the anxiety on the runway as we waited for the small plane back to Nairobi from the airstrip of a neighbouring camp, where my wife had been treated for breathing problems by a kindly nurse who had kept saying, "She will be alright," and had asked me to check the labelling of the medicines he was administering. Oh, and the solo pilot of our bush-hopping plane, who landed on the wrong airstrip because of the bad weather and only after having first aborted his landing when a herd of wildebeest crossed our runway.

However, in between the unease and the sweaty terror, we witnessed some of the most extraordinary wildlife displays our planet has to offer: two cheetahs taking down and then eating an impala beside the river; a leopardess playing with her cub in the morning rain; two month old lion cubs teaching each other to climb a tree; a male lion dragging a wildebeest kill half a kilometre or more to the safety of a rocky slope, out of reach of the hungry hyenas and jackals. But even amid all this majesty and wonder, I was most excited by the bird life!

Eagles, owls, storks, flycatchers and cranes – almost wherever we drove with our dedicated guide, Charles, there was a new species to see and photograph. I spotted four different types of woodpecker (including the **Nubian (21cm)** (see page 12) variety in its pale green and red), five different vulture species, and those brands of plover that were variously dressed in smart or spectacular outfits. I photographed a Purple Grenadier with its red beak and eye-ring, cinnamon head and purple tummy, and the cheeky-looking **D'Arnaud's Babet (16-19cm)**, which popped in and out of view as we watched lions stir from their day's sleep in the early evening. A **Hildebrandt's Starling (18cm)** distracted me as we observed a male elephant grazing a tree, and the late sun caught its blue and orange feathers as it clasped a stone in its beak. Was it building a nest? Whatever its motivation, the starling presented an engaging and unusual portrait. There's beauty in simplicity but there's no hiding the excitement of photographing activity – it can make for a more interesting image.

A Silverbird, painted in halves of orange and silver, sang in a low-slung tree close to our tent. We watched a **Yellow-billed Oxpecker (20cm)** go to work on the ear of a tolerant Buffalo down by the river, stripping its mighty host of fleas. Oxpeckers are blood-loving birds and while they consume ticks filled with the liquid, they eat straight from an animal's own supply, too, digging at a wound until it oozes with food. Nearby, a **Village Weaver (15-17cm)** was building its nest above a river heaving with hippos. The male bird hopes to attract a female with his intricately constructed home, but if he fails he will destroy his own work and begin again in a poignant bid to be successful next time.

During an evening drive, a **Coqui Francolin (28cm)** emerged from behind a mound of earth, and the light brought out its orange neck and face against a lime green backdrop. On our first day of safari, a Kori Bustard fixed us with a suspicious stare from the bush in the heat of the afternoon as we were driven from the grassy airstrip to our camp.

Lilac-breasted Roller, Masai Mara, Kenya

opposite: Hildebrandt's Starling,
Masai Mara, Kenya

above: D'Arnaud's Babet,
Masai Mara, Kenya

opposite: Yellow-billed Oxpecker,
Masai Mara, Kenya

top: Village Weaver,
Masai Mara, Kenya;

right: Coqui Francolin,
Masai Mara, Kenya

above: Northern White-crowned Shrike

opposite top: Von der Decken's Hornbill

opposite bottom left: Sooty Chat

opposite bottom right: Southern Ground Hornbill,
all Masai Mara, Kenya

The male, which weighs roughly twice as much as the female, is said to be the heaviest bird capable of flight in the world. Not a bad claim to fame! Kori Bustards live on the ground and are described as opportunistic omnivores. The males try to breed with as many females as they can and then take no part in the parenting. Hmm. Sadly, and unlike in my photograph of the francolin, the background in my best bustard image was a tangled mess of foliage and undergrowth. Composition matters! You can get away with a muddled photograph if you're truly showing a bird in its 'environment', but more often than not I'm left feeling disappointed.

A **Northern White-crowned Shrike (19-23cm)** perched obligingly on the shortened branch of a tree

close to the dining area of our camp and, further out, a **Sooty Chat (15-16cm)** glanced upwards against an olive background, all black, apart from the merest hint of a white patch on its mid-wing. And as we drove towards a pair of female cheetahs painstakingly preparing for a hunt on a golden evening, we encountered the rather unfortunate looking but nonetheless magnificent **Southern Ground Hornbill (90-129cm)**. This is the largest species in the hornbill group, and males can reach well over a metre in length and can weigh more than 6kg. It is an intimidating bird, and reptiles as well as mammals, including hares, would be well advised to stay out of its path. The patches of red bare skin on its head and neck are thought to protect its eyes from dust as it forages for food on the ground during the dry

season, but give it the appearance of a character in a horror movie. It is roughly twice the size of the more attractive **Von der Decken's Hornbill (35cm)** that we eyed hopping along the bush. A male bird, with a red and orange beak, he cut quite a dash going about his business cloaked in black and white plumage.

Not until my wife became unwell and we found ourselves en route to a medical centre in the neighbouring Masai Mara National Reserve did we spot the magnificent **Grey Crowned Cranes (100cm).** Hurtling along a bumpy track, my wife gave very short shrift to the idea of stopping to photograph these birds that I'd longed to see on safari. We did encounter them again during an afternoon in Nairobi's National Park, although only at a frustrating distance. Their red, white and black faces are studded with blue eyes that somehow seem perpetually surprised, and their heads are crowned by feathers that might look more at home on the back of a hedgehog. Notice, too, the red inflatable throat pouch.

Back in the Olare Motorogi Conservancy, a White-browed Coucal made an appearance, impressively silhouetted with its prominent tail feathers against a grey sky, but damp from a morning shower. A Rufous-naped Lark, one of two or three lark species to grace our trip, just about managed to reveal its subtle but pretty features in the gloom. Males sometimes put on conspicuous displays by fluttering their wings from prominent perches, but whatever the gender of the bird I paused to photograph, it seemed uninspired by our presence.

Despite this roll call of beauty, however, not a single bird on our trip could compete with the Lilac-breasted Roller itself. As I have already mentioned, I had seen the species in South Africa, but many years earlier, and I was determined to take a striking photograph of a Kenyan bird. One sun-drenched evening, Charles parked the van on the edge of an escarpment. The weather had been wet, so the plain that stretched out before us seemed particularly vibrant, lit gold by the light. We were in lion territory, though, and I was on high alert. Earlier in the day we had spotted a lion making its way along the ridge of just such a hill. As we climbed higher, I watched my step, too, mindful that two days earlier we had encountered an African rock python lazing in the sun.

Wildebeest grazed below us and impala eyed us nervously from just behind the crest of the elevation. As we made our return, unharmed, to our vehicle, I noticed a Lilac-breasted Roller (see frontis) sitting on a tree in the late rays of the day. It was the ideal light to bring out its colours in their full, iridescent glory. The sun illuminated the greens and blues, the turquoise, pinks and purples. I didn't manage to draw as close as I would have liked, but I managed to take a sharp shot of it against a hybrid backdrop of greens and browns. What a sighting! I'd photographed one days earlier, but there was something very special about the colouring of this roller. Its beauty, however, would have been lost on the insects and small vertebrates on which the species feeds. If you're too big to be eaten on the ground, you will be carried back to the branch of a tree, where this heavenly looking bird will tear you apart before dining on your flesh.

Grey Crowned Cranes, Nairobi
National Park, Kenya

AFRICAN PENGUIN (60-70cm)

Think penguins and the mind naturally wanders to the coldest climes on the planet. Africa's only penguin, however, does not rely on freezing temperatures. The African Penguin, also known as the 'Jackass Penguin', thanks to the rather inelegant noises it makes that resemble a donkey's bray, is roughly half the size of the world's tallest species of penguin. The Emperor, star of David Attenborough's *Dynasties* series, stands at more than a metre tall. Disarming in the way they waddle along the beach, flippers outstretched, as you might hope, African Penguins are black and white with a touch of pink above the eye. I watched a colony of these charming birds around forty kilometres from Cape Town at Boulders Beach in Simon's Town.

In the area for my brother's wedding, my wife and I drove out across the mountains on a hot day under rich blue skies. It's an odd experience watching these rare, incredible birds for the first time, as one stands shoulder to shoulder with fellow tourists. The penguins station themselves on either side of the boardwalk, sunbathing and preening each other, obvious targets for the busy camera phones pointed in their direction. A handful were silhouetted on the edge of rocks against the sky, while others swam in the turquoise sea where they are protected from aerial threats by their black coats that merge with the water when viewed from above, and from marine predators by their white underparts. This is called countershading, and the Atlantic Puffins that we encountered in an earlier chapter benefit from the same method of camouflage.

The hot beach was crowded with penguins, and I photographed three emerging from the water in a staggered line. When you're confronted by a photogenic species or easily accessible spectacle, it helps to be original in the way you compose your image. It could set your photography apart. And, even if you are a photographer first and foremost, don't forget to spend some time just looking and admiring. It's not all about the photography.

African Penguins feed on small fish such as anchovies and sardines, but also on squid and crustaceans. Devastatingly, we learned in 2010 that populations of this precious bird had declined by 95% since pre-industrial times, and there seems to be a real risk of extinction due to factors including climate change, oil spills, overfishing and the destruction of their habitats.

opposite and right:
African Penguins, Boulders Beach,
Cape Peninsula, South Africa

MARABOU STORK (152cm)

The Marabou Stork is ugly. It's even known as the 'undertaker bird' on account of its appearance from behind. Its head, like those of vultures, lacks feathers, which would otherwise become matted with the blood of the carcasses it scavenges. It is a huge bird but particularly so in flight. Its wingspan typically measures between 2.1 and 2.8 metres, which is impressive, though still some way off the Andean Condor, and smaller still than the world's longest-winged bird, the Wandering Albatross.

What's immediately striking about the Marabou Stork on the ground is the pink gular sac that hangs from its throat – an area of featherless skin that marks it out as a peculiar-looking creature. I photographed several of these wading birds grouped together in Nairobi National Park. I'd seen them first in the Mara, where I also watched Black Storks flying over a cheetah kill and spotted White Storks too. If, like me, you haven't been lucky enough to catch sight of a White Stork straying far from home over the English countryside, maybe you've seen one nesting on the roof of a house in continental Europe?

OSTRICH (2.1-2.8m)

Driving through Nairobi National Park on the outskirts of the city with our guide, Francis, we encountered these extraordinary birds grazing the savannah. The males were flush with a glossy black coat, shaggy white tail and pink head, beak and neck, while the female bird was a drabber, muted version, a mix of greys and browns. I'd seen Ostriches in South Africa's Pilanesberg National Park in my late teens, and again from the air on our way to our Mara camp. But now I was better equipped to convey something of the sheer peculiarity of these creatures.

Looking at them, you would have no sense that Ostriches are the planet's fastest birds on land, capable of astonishing speeds of around 70 kilometres per hour. Quite a feat, given they are also the largest (weighing up to 145kg and reaching heights of up to nearly three metres) and, arguably, clunkiest looking of the world's birds.

Although, rather endearingly, Ostriches can escape attack not just by running away but also by lying flat on the ground and hiding, they're able to kick out violently with their long, strong legs, too. They are said to live in nomadic groups of between five and fifty birds, and territorial males can fight for the rights to a harem of between two and seven females.

We weren't blessed with sunny weather in the park, and I had to be creative in my compositions. I photographed the male with the female behind – in the picture it is as if one bird has two necks – and ended up cropping another of my shots to emphasise the length and quirkiness of a single Ostrich neck.

If you think of Ostriches as almost more animal than bird, you might not be shocked to discover that the male has a retractable 'copulatory organ' that measures roughly 20cm and that, unlike all other living birds, both genders apparently relieve themselves separately of urine and faeces. Who knew? Something to try not to think about if you ever find yourself eating Ostrich meat, as I did in the form of meatballs in a Nairobi restaurant after our afternoon's safari.

Ostrich, Nairobi National Park,
Kenya

Owls

Did you know that the famous tu-whit tu-whoo of the Tawny Owl is in fact an exchange between two owls? But there is a mystery to owls beyond this rather surprising fact, thanks to their largely nocturnal habits. Their call through the dark trees above and around us can be reassuring or menacing, depending on your mood.

My childhood sightings of owls were only of shadowy Tawnies in the dimming or darkened evening and I'm not even sure I've seen one in good light to this day. A sketchy sighting of a Scops Owl in the twilight was also all I managed after a determined search in the grounds of a former nunnery in the Corsican summer of 2016. And while I did have a better view of an Eagle Owl as a seventeen year-old on South African safari when it became briefly transfixed by the ranger's headlights, I have only recently begun to take advantage of the diurnal habits of several species of owl.

If all you've ever seen of an owl is a black shape in the gathering gloom, I have news for you. More than you might think, owls hunt in the daylight too. The Short-eared Owl is a fine example. As I've made my way from reserve to reserve, I've enjoyed a series of encounters with this loping predator. At RSPB Pulborough in Sussex, I watched as two or three hunted low over the wetlands in the middle of a bright, sunny day. At Wicken Fen in Cambridgeshire, too, one flew so close I was able to photograph its languid shape above the fields – though not in sufficient detail for this book!

While owls' disc-like faces and night vision set them apart, they are, at heart, raptors – and no less compelling to watch as they hunt for prey in Britain and beyond. Although their eyes can't move in their sockets, owls are able to turn their heads about 270 degrees if they want to have a look at what's going on behind them. Keep an eye out yourself as you take an early morning or late evening stroll in the countryside or even a town park. And keep an ear out too.

opposite: Barn Owl, Hertfordshire

overleaf: Little Owl, Buckinghamshire

LITTLE OWL (21-23cm)

I think, but I can't be sure, that I first spotted a Little Owl on a fence post in the Tuscan twilight. We were driving across a stunning landscape to supper in one of our favourite restaurants. It's a special and familiar stretch of remote countryside with views of Mount Amiata looming distantly above the cypress-lined road. We've seen baby boar feeding in the field just metres from our car along the same route and paused to watch the sun dipping below the horizon. I merely caught a brief glimpse of the tiny owl on the evening in question but my later research suggested that it was unlikely to have been any other species.

Only after one of my listeners posted a photograph on Instagram of a resident Little Owl in a London park, however, could I be absolutely sure that I'd seen one of these little hunters. Following Sue's directions, I waited as the light darkened on a February evening and photographed a grumpy-looking bird as it went about its business in the gloom. I returned a few days later in the hope of finding it out and about in more generous light but the owl winking at me from between the branches of a tree is frustratingly dimly lit.

Still after the 'perfect shot', I was given a tour of the same park by Paula, a photographer who has spent many hours immersed in the sights and sounds of the place and can distinguish the call of the owl amongst the din of the Ring-necked Parakeets. We visited as the sun came up and were greeted by a cacophony of colour. A golden ball of orange and yellow lit up the mist above the ponds as a heron fished in its rays. What a special time dawn can be! Birds are perhaps even more active at the start of the day than they are in the evening. Eventually, after several hours of hard looking, Paula spotted a Little Owl in a distant tree with her binoculars but I was only close enough for an 'environment' shot.

I haven't mentioned the name of the park because there is always a risk with such iconic species that too much attention could push them from their precious territories. Introduced to this country in the 19th century, the Little Owl population in the UK is estimated to have fallen by almost a quarter between 1995 and 2008. Still, keep your eye out for these pocket-sized, highly territorial hunters during daylight hours as they are not only nocturnal in their activities. They keep an eye out for prey from their perch and their diet includes small mammals, birds, beetles and worms. Excess food is, I've read, stored in hiding places. Which is rather clever!

Just before this book went to press, and desperate for a printable picture of the species, I googled how best to see a Little Owl. The first result that came up was Neil Neville Photography. Neil runs a hide near Slough in the Buckinghamshire countryside and within a fortnight, hidden in a camouflaged wooden structure, the two of us were chatting away as we waited in hope for a local male to fly down from his oak tree to feed on the mealworms Neil had put out for him. Yes, I was paying for the privilege, but this was a chance to watch and photograph an elusive species at close quarters. The owl obliged us several times as he journeyed to and fro between the perching posts provided and his wife, who was sitting on a clutch of eggs back in the oak tree.

BARN OWL (33-39cm)

My mother longs to see her first Barn Owl. That she is still waiting despite the quickness of her eye and her love of nature, is an indication of just how rare – and special – these twilight hunters are. During a gap in the BBC reporter rota (which briefly ruled my life in the winter of early 2013) I set out for some precious time alone in Wales. Arriving after midnight, I was met by a bank of snow that buried the steep ascent to the house. I tucked myself in for the night and hoped snowflakes would continue to fall as I slept.

Finding myself snowed in the following morning evoked happy childhood memories. Even modern Britain is occasionally forced to bow to the elements and those few days were memorable as I made the most of the white landscapes rolled out before me. I walked the thirty minutes to town for provisions but when the sun began to clear the way, I headed for the higher hills in my car.

As the road curved away towards the Berwyns my eye was distracted by movement in the hedgerow. A Barn Owl! The chances of bumping into one like this were small. Remote, really. And so this was my first. The cold weather had forced the bird out into the middle of the day and it flitted from low slung tree to tree, gloriously pale brown and white against the even whiter snow. I have since photographed Barn Owls at both Wicken Fen and Otmoor but to see one outside the safer confines of a reserve made this sighting extra special.

Barn Owls' acute hearing and light sensitive eyes allow them to hunt for tiny mice, voles and shrews in the dead of night. They can even locate a meal with precision through hearing alone. Sounds are funnelled towards their ears, which are located asymmetrically just behind the eyes, by the distinctive facial disc. Once Barn Owls have captured prey in their deadly talons, they don't tend to hang around and normally swallow the hapless little creature whole before later coughing up pellets of bone and fur. Larger mammals and small birds can also fall victim to these expert hunters.

If you're lucky enough to see a Barn Owl – and they're immediately distinguishable from other owls by their pale shape – remember how brilliantly adapted they are to their lifestyles. Their unusually soft feathers, though unsuited to rain, enable almost silent flight as they approach their prey with trademark stealth. The bird I watched hunting low over the Cambridgeshire Fens flew like a ghost in the afternoon light. Just as hares grace our fields, so Barn Owls embellish our skies, gliding ethereally from meal to meal.

I have my wife to thank for the picture in this book. After she pointed out a video of Little Owls on the BBC News website, I tracked down the cameraman, Russell Savory, on social media. Generously, Russell agreed to pick me up from a supermarket car park outside Bishop's Stortford and take me to a field where he had set up a makeshift hide from which to watch and photograph the local Barn Owls. It was January and the light died early, but not before I had captured this magnificent bird, backlit against the fleeting sun.

Birds of Prey

The most magnificent birds in the sky, raptors capture our imagination through the ferocity of their hunting, the speed of their flight and the span of their wings. They are the undisputed lords and ladies of their habitats, and perch, hover or swoop at the pinnacle of the avian hierarchy. From the mighty splendour of the Golden Eagle to the stealth of the miniature Merlin, a mere quarter of its size, birds of prey rule their landscapes.

There are sixteen breeding species in the UK and I have seen fifteen. Which, yes, leaves one. Now that I have seen the ghostly Montagu's Harrier on safari in Kenya (there are only a handful of breeding pairs in Britain), all that remains is the Goshawk. And that's not for the want of trying. Trips to Lake Vyrnwy in Wales and the Forest of Dean in England have proved fruitless. Gliding as it does through dense trees, the Goshawk is a reclusive species that reveals itself fleetingly in a brief spring spell when partners put on a majestic display above the canopy – or so I've heard! So powerful are its beak and talons that it has been known to take an adult Buzzard, and yet the male is not much larger than a female Sparrowhawk.

While my preoccupation with birds has, for many years now, broadened and deepened beyond the raptor's reach, I will never tire of the thrill of spotting an eagle, a harrier or a falcon going about its deadly business.

Tawny Eagle, Masai Mara, Kenya

RED-FOOTED FALCON (28-34cm)

During my mid teens I developed a lust for travel. I wanted to see the world and I wanted to see more of it than anyone else. It's an itch I haven't entirely scratched, so in 2016 I asked my builder to show me the country of his birth. Kujdesi, now a good friend, arrived here from Albania twenty years ago and runs a thriving construction business.

The two of us decamped to the Balkans for a long May weekend and drove from the capital, Tirana – Kujdesi's hometown – through northern, sunlit Kosovo, up over the Montenegrin mountains and finally down to the red roofs of Dubrovnik. Along the way, we met cows in the road, drove through a frightening rainstorm – water smashing against the windscreen – and threw snowballs in no-man's land between Kosovo and Montenegro. We ate fish above the lake where Kujdesi had rowed his boat as a boy, and I photographed a Corn Bunting in the uplands of northern Albania. My hopes, however, of notching up new species at a promising bird reserve on the other side of the Montenegrin mountains were washed out by the whipping rain.

Back in Albania after our whirlwind road trip and after a traditional, home-cooked breakfast, we headed south to the old town of Berat, which was designated a UNESCO World Heritage site in 2008. We climbed up to the ruined fortress that affords views over the city streets spread out below. The scenery was pleasant enough and the sun took turns with the clouds above the green fields of the distant valley. But what really caught my eye was a kestrel-like bird, only thinner, zipping between the sparse trees that studded the hillside. Its wings were more delicately drawn than any hawk I'd seen before and I knew instinctively that this was something to be excited about.

Only later, with the help of Mike, my birdwatcher friend in Wales, who examined the photograph I took, did I realise my discovery: a Red-footed Falcon. What an elegant, handsome bird! It's a rare visitor to Britain, so there was considerable excitement at the news that one was in the area the same day I was in the Somerset Levels listening out for Cuckoos. Fractionally bigger than a Merlin, the Albanian bird was probably a female, on account of its pale underparts, although I can't rule out the possibility that it was a juvenile male. The joys and uncertainties of birdwatching!

The adult male is largely sooty grey with a mix of reds and oranges and yellows marking out its eye ring, talons, shins, underbelly, undertail and the base of its beak. I was too far away to have taken an image to be proud of, and the bird blurred against the mountainous backdrop. There is, nonetheless, a strange satisfaction to be had from looking at pictures online (or in books) of birds immediately after spotting them for the first time. It's almost as if you're buying shares in their uniqueness.

KESTREL (32-35cm)

Only the Merlin and the Hobby are smaller British birds of prey. Kestrels are relatively common and a familiar sight as they hover on the sides of motorways looking for mice and other small animals. Like miniature helicopters, they are distinctive in the air and the male is a proud-looking bird with a slate-grey head, rich brown back and yellow front, with flecks of black adding texture to its body and wings. The slightly larger females are less striking, but I had fun photographing one on the grasslands of Wicken Fen in Cambridgeshire. There are, according to the RSPB, approaching fifty thousand pairs in the UK and they are unfussy about the landscapes they hunt.

Lesser Kestrels are, as their name might suggest, smaller than Kestrels, but I still agonised for some time over the identity of the birds nesting in the clock tower of an old nunnery I was staying in on the island of Corsica. I'm almost certain they were Lesser Kestrels – which aren't found on British shores –

because they came out to hunt as it grew dark, no doubt snatching insects in the lamplight, and they did seem slimmer and smaller than the common Kestrel. I also laid eyes on the Lesser species high in the Indian sky in the jungle outside Mumbai, thanks to the keen eye and identification skills of Dan, the British bird enthusiast who was staying in the same tree house hotel as I was. Thrilled though I was by these sightings, it would be wrong to be dismissive of our Kestrel. Hovering expertly and at great length above the fields and hills of Britain, it is an accomplished hunter and elegant on the eye.

Kestrel, Wicken Fen, Cambridgeshire

MONTAGU'S HARRIER (43-47cm)

Even rarer in the UK than the Hen Harrier is the Montagu's Harrier. There are thought to be only a handful of breeding pairs here and their whereabouts are kept secret when possible, so the prospect of ever setting eyes on one of these stylish birds is remote. I did have high hopes in Sardinia when I drove for several hours in search of their habitat on the west coast of the island but returned to the villa we were staying in having had to make do with sightings of flamingos and Marsh Harriers.

In January 2018, however, on our three day safari in Kenya's Olare Motorogi Conservancy that lies to the west of Nairobi, I had my chance. Along with the mighty Martial Eagle, a pair of which had nested locally, and the gorgeous African Fish Eagle, Montagu's Harriers were said to be a possibility. We never did catch a glimpse of the Martial Eagle and we had to wait for our afternoon in Nairobi National Park to spot the Fish Eagle, but suddenly, as we were picking out hornbills in the trees, Charles, our guide, excitedly pointed towards a pair of distant grey shapes. Could these be Montagu's Harriers, birds that had captured my imagination thirty years earlier in my mini Collins guide? Disappointingly not. They were, instead, pretty, arrow-like **Black-shouldered**

Kites (35cm), a species I would photograph the following year with their piercing red eyes in South Africa at both Strandfontein and Babylonstoren.

We didn't give up hope of spotting a Montagu's, though, and the following morning we found a male hunting its territory. He dipped low before rising again, fanning his tail in flight. What a moment! The raptor was too busy in its movements for us to be able to get close enough for a detailed picture but there's at least a hint of lyricism to the only shot I took worth reproducing. An impala sits impassively in the damp, and atop a tree in the middle-ground are two kestrels – whose identity as Lesser Kestrels I only recognised when I looked at the picture! Frustratingly, we did encounter a female Montagu's Harrier at tantalisingly close quarters later in the trip but that was while we were en route to the very basic medical centre at which my wife was treated, and she was not amused when I tentatively suggested we stop briefly to photograph the bird.

If you're ever lucky enough to see a Montagu's Harrier in this country, the male is just about distinguishable from the Hen thanks mainly to the black stripe across its inner wing that shows in flight.

HEN HARRIER (44-52cm)

I've incorporated the Hen Harrier into this book even though I have never taken a photograph of one that merits inclusion, because the seeing of it was so flesh-tinglingly exciting and because I don't think there is a more precious breeding bird in Britain. Nor any more graceful. To gaze on, as a male – pale grey against the gathering gloom – flies into roost in long reed beds, is to witness an ethereal scene.

Once, high up on the outskirts of Snowdonia, I was convinced the dark brown bird hovering in the neck of the hill was a female Hen. When it turned out to be a Buzzard, my determination to see one of these ravishing raptors with my own eyes became almost

an obsession, and I searched Google for likely spots within striking distance of home. I even overnighted in Cley next the Sea on a trip to Cley Marshes, the famous National Trust reserve in Norfolk. But while I glimpsed – for the first time – a Hobby disturbing the waterfowl and watched **Marsh Harriers (48-56cm)** as they hunted in the distance, the Hen Harrier, our most intensively persecuted bird of prey, eluded me.

Admittedly, I hadn't seen a Marsh Harrier before, so it was brilliant to watch a young bird with a golden crown nibble at a carcass in the marshes. I've seen several since – not just at my regular Otmoor haunt

but also in Sardinian wetlands – although these birds, while highly visible on reserves, are usually shy enough to withdraw just out of easy range of my long lens. The best photograph I've managed was a distant shot of a male, handsome in its understated blend of golds, silvers, browns and russets and set against a Somerset farmhouse near to where it was hunting the wetlands.

Having missed the Hen Harriers at Cley, I hoped instead for success at Pulborough, the RSPB reserve which would yield my first Nightingale months later. But no luck there either. Driven now by the itch of failure, I lost myself – literally for a while – in the Sussex hills, as I hopelessly scanned the sky for hours.

Eventually, my research threw up the wonders of Wicken Fen, another National Trust Reserve, this time in Cambridgeshire, not far from Ely. Back in the car, my carbon footprint dragging behind me, I set off with renewed hope. Sightings at the Fen were said to be regular and the odds were in my favour.

The harriers weren't due until twilight so I walked the neighbouring Fens during the afternoon, before winding my way back towards their favoured reed beds. I'd spotted what I thought was a Merlin along the way and as day edged towards night, a white ghost-like shape stooped low over the fields. A Barn

Owl. This was becoming one of those unusual, utterly joyful afternoons. But I hadn't driven a hundred miles for Barn Owls – or even Merlins.

It became the perfect day when the milky grey of a male Hen Harrier swooped in over the trees and moved to and fro above the reeds. One of this country's rarest wildlife displays was unfolding in the dusk. I wanted to shout out in happiness. A Ringtail, as the female and immature birds are known, also flew in to find a bed for the night and revealed the eponymous white ring on her tail.

I've returned to Wicken Fen several times since and seen the Hen Harriers again, although my photographs have never done justice to their eery beauty in the darkening countryside. And on a recent trip to Mid Wales, a male flew out in front of our car as we drove through the upland moors near Lake Bala in late April. The bird had returned to its breeding grounds and there was something particularly exciting about seeing the species in its upland habitat.

clockwise, from top left:
Marsh Harrier, Somerset

Black-shouldered Kite, Western Cape, South Africa

Montagu's Harrier, Masai Mara, Kenya

COMMON BUZZARD (51-57cm)

Common Buzzards make me think of the Welsh valley I spent so much time in as a boy and still visit as often as I can. There's something mournful about these birds of prey as they circle heavenwards above the fields and call out plaintively across the hills. Birds can help to give an identity to a place with their aerial presence and the noises that they make. They can define its atmosphere and influence the way we feel about the landscape.

Buzzards are, according to the RSPB, now our most common British raptor, and the charity estimates the number of breeding pairs at between 57-79,000, although a farmer I know wonders whether Red Kites have begun to push local birds from their territories. I hope not. Happily, I recently watched a newly fledged Buzzard make its way from conifer to conifer, close to a nest I'd learned of, just down the lane from my parents' house.

Despite their relative abundance, however, Buzzards are difficult to photograph. They're often high in the sky and when I've spotted one sitting on a fence post or pylon, it has seemed shy and suspicious of movement. I did, though, successfully photograph a bird coming into land on a wooden mast in Somerset after searching for a Glossy Ibis at an RSPB reserve.

Much rarer in Britain than our Common Buzzards are Honey Buzzards. I've never seen them here but first spotted the species soaring on distant thermals in northern Italy and then flying above Table Mountain in Cape Town, and in Malta. They feed principally on the larvae of wasps and bees and their grey head and yellow eye must be arresting up close. The length of the head helps to distinguish the bird in flight from the Common Buzzard.

More colourful than either species is the **Jackal Buzzard (44-55cm)**. I crept near enough through the Cape vineyards to capture the ruddy and white chest, black head and white wing bar of this multi-coloured raptor, as it sat on a tree stripped of its leaves. If you ever find yourself looking up at a Jackal Buzzard in flight, the prominent white expanses on its underwing are a useful give-away.

opposite: Common Buzzard,
Somerset

ROUGH-LEGGED BUZZARD (50-60cm)

My first long distance twitch was a triumph. Beyond anything I could have imagined. I can't now remember how I learned that a Rough-legged Buzzard was hunting on an Essex golf course on the east coast, but it might have been on Twitter, where there are plenty of bird alert accounts you can follow, if you ever catch the bug.

Of the three buzzard species found in the UK, by far the most common is – wait for it – the Common Buzzard. I know it's shallow, but I struggle to get excited by these familiar raptors that wheel, often in pairs, higher and higher in the sky. They can also be annoyingly easy to mistake for a rarer bird and this has led to disappointment in the past. The Rough-legged, on the other hand, is a species I'd wanted to see almost since a fascination with birdwatching had first stirred in me as a boy.

Explaining the point of twitching to the uninitiated – and even to myself at times! – can be a challenge. Driving sometimes hundreds of miles at short notice just to add a bird to a list that might never be read by anyone else… Why? What *is* the point? Well, it's not just about the list. There's an almost indescribable thrill to seeing a bird that you've never seen before. Particularly if it's rare, and even more particularly if you've dreamed for years of laying eyes on it. And there's the adrenaline involved, too, in not knowing whether you'll get to a location in time.

I arrived in Clacton-on-Sea just as the autumn sun was losing its strength. There's often a nerve-wracking walk – or run – to be negotiated before catching up with other birders making their way back to their cars. Has the bird already flown? Has the drama already reached its climax? West London to the east coast is a long way to go for nothing more than the late afternoon sun on the water.

I was in luck, it seemed. The bird was still around, though it had most recently been sighted on a distant fence post. I ran on, still unsure whether I'd be in time, before slowing to a walk as I neared a dwindling collection of birders staring intently through telescopes. There it was! Not much more than a speck. I would, just about, have been content with that. But soon what turned out to be a juvenile bird flew in our direction and I was rewarded with an early evening hunting session.

How strange to watch such a wild, rare creature search for food against a backdrop of tiled roofs and high rise buildings. But, as I mentioned in my Waxwing profile, unusual visitors often turn up in unexpected surroundings and this buzzard didn't seem to mind the audience it had drawn from miles around. It almost seemed to be courting us. Thanks to the angle of the low evening sun, which caught the bird's underparts as it hovered above the long grass, my photographs turned out well. A bonus! Indisputably worth the petrol money, although we twitchers have to ask ourselves an obvious question: does the pursuit of nature justify our carbon footprint?

Very few Rough-legged Buzzards make it to Britain, and those that do winter here aren't always immediately distinguishable from the Common Buzzard, whose plumage can vary from bird to bird. The Rough-legged does tend to be paler than its sister species and it spends longer hovering in search of food. The east coast of England seems to be a favoured landing spot for wintering birds but you'd be lucky to bump into one. If you do manage to achieve as good a view as I did, then the more heavily feathered legs might help you tell it apart from the Common Buzzard. Keep an eye out on Twitter from October through to April for news of these magnificent migrants.

Rough-legged Buzzard,
Clacton-on-Sea, Essex

RED KITE (60-66cm)

There's not just mystery in rarity, there's beauty too. When I was growing up, Red Kites were confined to a magical pocket of mid-Wales. To have seen one then really would have been a treat. I didn't. They seemed, to a young boy, an impossibly long car journey away. But some time after their reintroduction into southern England and Scotland, I did watch a solitary bird soar above our own Welsh valley. Rather like seeing a fox in the countryside remains a thrill despite the animal's overrunning of London's lamplit streets, witnessing this magnificent bird in the 'wild' was an entirely different experience to catching regular sight of the scavenger through the car windscreen on the M40.

These red and white raptors were driven to the very point of extinction in Britain by the 1970s. But between 1989 and 1994 they were reintroduced by conservationists, with birds from Sweden, Spain and even one from Wales released as far afield as the Chilterns and northern Scotland. The project proved a huge success, and Kites soon began breeding both north and south of Hadrian's Wall.

Today, if you find yourself between London and Oxford, take the time if you can to leave the motorway at Junction 6 and make your way to the pretty little town of Watlington. There you can stand and marvel as Red Kites swoop, sometimes to shop level on the high street. Even on a grey day, they're quite a sight, and when the sun catches a kite, its feathers glow orange and red and the bird shimmers in the sky.

Just up the road is Watlington Hill, standing guard over the flat, sprawling Oxfordshire countryside. As you climb its chalky slopes, dozens of kites will glide and dive above and beneath you. There are few, if any, spots more generous to the bird photographer. Just be still and patient and the birds will come to you. With wingspans of up to five and a half feet, they are not much less broad than the mighty Golden Eagle, but in spring they are comfortably lighter in weight than a Mallard Duck.

Don't confuse the floating beauty of Red Kites with friendliness. Capture their yellow eyes on camera and you'll see at once that these are monsters of the clouds. There is ferocity in their pupils and although they're largely content with plucking carrion from the landscape, they can kill mice and other small mammals, too.

The obstacle to taking a rewarding shot of a Red Kite is that you're usually photographing them from below, their shapes silhouetted against the sky, and I've had to brighten some of my pictures to breathe the lavish colours back into their feathers. The birds rarely seem to settle on a perch and when they do, it's not easy to sneak to within range without them lifting off again. The pictures I've used for this book were taken on a family-run farm near the market town of Rhayader in Mid Wales. The farmer puts out meat for the birds daily and I photographed them as they came in to feed.

Don't forget, however successful you've been, to put your camera down for a while in the company of these magnificent raptors. To look on as they glide above the British countryside and scavenge for their next meal, is to remember that this is an experience that almost became extinct here within my lifetime.

opposite and overleaf: Red Kite, Rhayader, Mid Wales

SHORT-TOED SNAKE EAGLE (62-67cm)

When I first saw a Short-toed Snake Eagle hunting above the vineyards of a valley that rises up to Montepulciano in the heart of the Tuscan countryside, I confused the brown and white raptor with the local Common Buzzards. Only when I inspected my grainy photos of the bird clinging to the top of a conifer, was I struck by its bright orange eye. What simply didn't occur to me even then, however, was that this medium-sized bird of prey could be an eagle, so much smaller did it seem than my mental image of what an eagle should look like. So when my friend Mike emailed back from Mid Wales with the unexpected news that I had, in fact, sent him a picture of a Short-toed Snake Eagle, I felt like I'd won an avian lottery.

The following summer I plunged into the ploughed earth of the fields running down from our hotel in the hope of photographing the eagle – and the European Bee-eaters that had also made the valley their home – up close. Despite the rather obvious thought that where there are snake eagles there are likely to be snakes, I was lost in the headspin of my ambition. Only at the end of the holiday did I ask the hotel manager about the risks I'd been taking. Her answer was alarming. Vipers, she informed me, liked to sunbathe on the churned earth of the rutted fields. One had even entered the kitchen that summer. Its bite, I learned, is lethal if you don't get the vaccine in time.

I'm still waiting for another Short-toed Snake Eagle to pose for me on a tree, but I have managed a reasonable shot of the bird in flight. The species often hunts from a height, and if you look up at an airborne Short-toed, you should notice the mainly white underparts that give way to a brownish chest and neck.

BLACK-CHESTED SNAKE EAGLE (63-68cm)

This was something special on a golden afternoon in the Mara. Charles, our Kenyan driver and expert spotter, caught sight of the magnificent bird of prey on a far-off tree. Like the big cats and hyenas, the raptors we saw on honeymoon didn't seem much bothered by our vehicle, so we were able to approach sufficiently close to the eagle for a clear image. There's always the chance the bird will fly before you can even raise your camera, but there's no point in taking a blurry photograph from a distance.

The Black-chested Snake Eagle is more eye-catching than the Short-toed Snake Eagle. Its dark chocolate chest feathers are distinctive and the white of its underbelly is pristine against the mix of browns and flecks of white of the upper wings. The yellow eye of the bird in my photograph is piercing as it catches the sunlight. Ours was a brief encounter but one that will endure in my memory.

BROWN SNAKE EAGLE (60-70cm)

We noticed this drab eagle perched high on a dead-looking tree, its feathers drenched in the East African morning rain. The Brown Snake Eagle lacks the more interesting plumage of its Short-toed and Black-chested relatives, but it is always a buzz to see a raptor for the first time, and this sighting added gloss to a morning in which we had watched a leopardess teach her daughter to hunt in the Mara. As its name suggests, the diet of the Brown Snake Eagle comprises largely of snakes and, thanks, we're told, to the protection afforded by its thick-skinned legs, it is capable of killing venomous species. Mambas and puffadders beware!

Black-chested Eagle, Masai Mara, Kenya

BATELEUR (55-70cm)

Our honeymoon in Kenya and Tanzania became, for me, as much about the birds as the animals. To that end we had requested a guide fully primed on the avian life of the Mara. Undeterred by the terrors of the nights and strengthened by African coffee, each dawn we would venture into the bush with Charles. As if the lions and leopards alone could not fill our eyes, we were greeted by close to one hundred and fifty species of birds during our three day safari. I was in bird heaven, and Charles and my wife generously indulged the near constant requests to, "Please stop, Charles!".

The Bateleur is a spectacular, though medium-sized eagle. Both male and female birds have striking orange-red facial masks that don't extend beyond the eye and they wear tunics of black, silver and chestnut with tawny wing coverts. The female is also the possessor of tawny secondary wing feathers. Bateleurs' tails are so unusually short that their talons stick out marginally behind them as they fly. We encountered a pair sitting calmly in a pine tree, entirely unbothered by our proximity. The two birds were totally silent as we observed them, neither uttering a bark or a scream, though they are capable of both. There was something endearing about this monogamous couple as they watched the world go by in the pale afternoon sun.

Bateleurs hunt birds such as doves and pigeons as well as small mammals and reptiles, but they're also effective scavengers and are said to be able to spot smaller carcases in advance of most of the competition. Impressively, they are thought to live to around 27 years old.

Bateleur, Masai Mara, Kenya

TAWNY EAGLE (60-75cm)

For all my excitement at spotting Black-chested as well as Brown Snake Eagles, vultures of five varieties and other raptors, too, the undisputed lord and lady of the Olare Motorogi Conservancy were the Tawny Eagles that met us around many a bend in the track. Large eagles, their plumage seemed to differ from bird to bird. Some were chocolate brown, almost from head to toe, others a silky golden hue. Whatever their colouring, though, they posed happily for us as we approached in our open-top truck.

The same sunlit evening that I saw that Lilac-breasted Roller, flush with purples, greens and blues in the late light after we had left the vehicle behind and trusted Charles (quite literally) with our lives, we watched a pair of Tawny Eagles putting on a dramatic display, one above the other. It was electrifying to witness them interacting high above our heads.

Tawnies inhabit much of the African continent, typically making their homes in dry landscapes, and also spread northeast to parts of Asia. They're known to steal food from weaker species of bird and their diet is diverse. They feed on a mix of mammals, lizards, birds and carrion. When we encountered a colony of petite, nervous (and extremely cute) pygmy mongoose, they seemed alerted to the presence of an approaching Tawny Eagle by the clamour of smaller birds in the neighbourhood.

At its plainest, the Tawny is an unspectacular bird, but in its twin plumage of browns and white golds, it boasts an obvious beauty. Just try not to mistake it for the very similar Steppe Eagle.

Tawny Eagle,
Masai Mara, Kenya

AFRICAN FISH EAGLE (63-75cm)

Ever since the then boyfriend of one of my cousins showed me a picture of an African Fish Eagle, I'd hoped to see one for myself. I asked Charles, our safari guide, to keep a particular eye out for these magnificent raptors as we made our way along the rivers of the Mara just outside the national reserve. But while we encountered Tawny Eagles, Bateleur, Lesser Kestrels, Black-shouldered Kites and even a Montagu's Harrier, we couldn't find our target. Having added over a hundred new species to my life list in three days and seen the Big Five at close quarters, too, I could hardly complain. But as we returned from Zanzibar to Kenya at the end of our honeymoon, I hoped that we might yet find the birds on a final afternoon's safari in Nairobi National Park.

The reserve is remarkable for its setting on the fringes of Nairobi itself. We watched towering giraffes take a stroll against the backdrop of distant skyscrapers and lions are known to hunt in the shadow of the city. My wife's uncle, Charlie, had posted a picture of the African Fish Eagle during a trip he had made to the same reserve earlier that year. His was a distant but lyrical image of a bird whose significance to me he couldn't have fully imagined when he took the photograph on his phone. We headed straight to a watering hole – an obvious habitat for the species – and before we had even quite reached it, my wife spotted one of the birds of my dreams fishing above the water.

None of my attempts at a close-up of the bird in flight quite worked. But in one shot, the eagle is dipping above some grazing impala, and I've been told that the picture looks like a painting. I'll settle for that. The white head, chestnut breast and dark brown body are all prominent. A truly breathtaking specimen.

As if finally laying eyes on my target species weren't sufficient excitement, that same afternoon we also witnessed an African Sacred Ibis preening the feathers of an African Spoonbill, watched a hippo rising from the water, and ate our packed lunch in the company of a crocodile that seemed uncomfortably close to our ramshackle van. There is nowhere that can match Africa for its wildlife, and few birds rival the African Fish Eagle.

African Fish Eagle, Nairobi National Park, Kenya

GOLDEN EAGLE (75-88cm)

By the time I turned eight, birds of prey already had me hooked. With their sharp talons, destructive beaks and sometimes giant wingspans, they captured my young imagination and fascinated me with their size and power. I have my uncle to thank for the introduction. Though I can't remember quite who or what first sparked my interest in the avian world, the trip I made to Scotland with my mum when I was seven to visit her younger brother was seminal. We took the sleeper train to Edinburgh and from there my uncle was charged with locating Golden Eagles and Ospreys for me to gaze at through boy-sized binoculars.

Then an academic at Edinburgh University, David looked after Peregrine Falcon nests for the RSPB in his spare time. It seemed to me to be an almost impossibly glamorous – not to say brave – job to protect the precious eggs from poachers and, of course, implied that he enjoyed regular sightings of the world's fastest fliers. But I was preoccupied with seeing for myself the most magnificent bird of all those to make the British Isles their home: the Golden Eagle.

Although the White-tailed Eagle, boasting even broader wings, might also lay claim to such a title, the Golden Eagle seemed to me to be the monarch of our skies. With a golden tint to the head feathers of an otherwise brown bird, and a wingspan the breadth of a tall man, its majesty is obvious.

Despite our best endeavours, however, we weren't able to catch more than a distant glimpse of the powerful predator after we parked on the side of the road. Even through my uncle's binoculars, it only emerged as a tiny dot on the grey skies leadening the foothills of the Highlands. But, thirty years on, I can still recall the moment. Such experiences act as pegs on which to hang memories (and we did also manage a closer encounter with a pair of juvenile Ospreys before they made the trip to Africa).

I have only seen a Golden Eagle once since. During a magical day on the Isle of Mull I spotted one soaring above the green of a hill, and photographed it high in a clear blue sky as it dwarfed the Common Buzzard it had for company. Although my views of the White-tailed Eagles I'd seen that morning had been at far closer quarters, there was a particular pleasure in identifying the bird in the glorious Scottish countryside.

Remarkably, given its bulk, the Golden Eagle is said to be able to reach speeds of more than 150 miles an hour in full stoop. Quite a turn of pace! Rabbits and birds such as Ptarmigan form part of this intimidating raptor's diet but although it is not unheard of for a bird to attack an adult deer, livestock are thought not to be at any great risk from a species whose territories can span 155 square kilometres.

Golden Eagles' eyries, built high on cliffs or in trees, are huge structures and, given that the birds can lay as many as four eggs, they need to be. Adults are romantic souls – they can remain monogamous throughout life-spans that stretch to thirty years – and they treat their parenting duties seriously too, taking it in turns to incubate the nest for up to six and a half weeks.

Sadly, while Golden Eagles once paraded English skies, today they are confined to the Highlands and Islands of Scotland and to Northern Ireland where they have been reintroduced. There was, famously, one male that continued to cling stubbornly to a rocky outcrop of the Lake District. Having made its home in Riggindale by Haweswater in Cumbria since 2001, it survived long after the death of its mate in 2004. Even that bird, though, seems finally to have died in 2016, which means, tragically, that within my lifetime the species has become extinct south of the Anglo-Scottish border.

It's up to us all to support the conservation of our most regal raptor and, at the very least, to ensure its survival in Scotland. Maybe one day this magisterial bird of prey might even find a home again in the mountains of England and Wales. For that to happen, suitable habitats may have to be reinstated and that might not be such a remote possibility. There seems to be a momentum gathering behind the principle of rewilding the British Isles.

WHITE-TAILED EAGLE (70-90cm)

From a very early age the White-tailed Eagle brought together everything that excited me about birds. Its monumental size together with its remote coastal habitat and the brilliant white of its head and tail, conjured something almost otherworldly in my young imagination. The species is now confined to remote parts of Scotland and it wasn't until my mid-thirties that I finally took to the motorways south and north of the border in pursuit of this giant fish-eating raptor.

I strapped myself in on a brilliantly hot and sunny day in the country lanes of Montgomeryshire, where I'd stopped off en route, and the skies stayed blue all the way up to the ferry crossing from the mainland at Oban. What incredible luck! With my car safely stowed on the deck below, I filled my eyes with the island views as we headed for Mull, perhaps the most famous British home of the magnificent White-tailed Eagle. The sun caught the waves as we made our approach and seabirds took advantage of the unusually balmy evening.

If you've never visited Mull – as I hadn't – it immediately strikes you as a special place. After a modest night in a rural B&B, I drove, with the roof down on my old Volkswagen, through the island to Ulva, the tiny harbour that serves the outer islands. Sheep ambled dreamily across the road and the weather held fair. The bracken was thick and green and the sea a rich blue between the headlands.

For a decade now, Martin Keivers has developed a relationship with the eagles. He runs Mull Charters and feeds them out at sea from his boat, a Lochin 33, during the spring, summer and early autumn months. Tourists assemble each morning near the quay. There were no guarantees – this is wildlife after all – but my hopes were high. All aboard, within minutes of the jetty Martin spotted a pair of White-tailed Eagles at home on one of the grassy outcrops of the neighbouring Isle of Ulva. Three decades in the making, this first sighting was an unforgettable experience.

Our trip just got better. Soon up to five birds took it in turns at intervals to circle our boat and pick their moment to plunge seawards towards the dead fish slung overboard. We were just metres from one of Scotland's most treasured species. Some of the birds had been ringed so that their movements could be tracked by ornithologists keen to understand more about their behaviour. At least one hadn't. Their eagle eyesight enables the birds to pick out the boat from miles away and we were treated to an astonishing display. Though there was perhaps something a little incongruous about such rare birds seeming so tame, the trust they had developed with Martin afforded us stunning opportunities to capture them in action.

The money shot, of course, is the moment the bird clutches the fish from the water. I didn't manage that, but I captured the eagles low over the sea in a variety of poses.

The White-tailed Eagle was hunted to extinction in the UK during the early 20th century and those we're lucky enough to enjoy today are the descendants of reintroduced birds. We must protect Britain's biggest bird so that future generations can marvel at its mighty beauty.

opposite: White-tailed Eagle, Isle of Mull, Scotland

LAPPET-FACED VULTURE (95-115cm)

It was a damp, greasy morning in the Olare Motorogi Conservancy, but that didn't seem to inhibit the wildlife. We had watched a male lion drag the half-devoured carcass of a wildebeest kill several hundred metres into the rocky hills and store it in bushes away from the prying eyes of jackals and strong-jawed hyenas. We had spotted my first Montagu's Harrier and Brown Snake Eagle, and photographed a hippopotamus jogging down to the river. Then something in the distance caught the eye of our guide, Charles. We drove closer and made out the first handful of vultures making a meal out of a zebra, prostrate on the savannah and made ill, perhaps, by the wet grass.

As we watched this grisly business unfold, more and more vultures descended on what we had at first assumed to be a corpse. Disturbingly, however, although the birds were tearing at its face, I suddenly noticed one of its legs move. To our surprise and horror, the zebra continued to

below and opposite: Lappet-faced Vulture, Masai Mara, Kenya

move the same limb at intervals. I hoped that this was some sort of post-death spasm and didn't want to believe my eyes. Charles, though, was transfixed and told us that he had never witnessed such a thing during his decade of showing wildlife enthusiasts around the Conservancy. The evidence, unfortunately, seemed irrefutable. This beautiful, black and white striped beast, was being eaten alive by birds that looked like they had just emerged from some ancient interpretation of hell. We had been heading back to camp for lunch but my stomach now began to protest. Watching a cheetah kill had been challenging enough but this was verging on the traumatic – not least of course for the poor zebra itself.

Among the gruesome crowd of mostly White-backed Vultures (I spotted a Hooded Vulture too), were at least two larger specimens in the shape of the Lappet-faced Vulture. These are such enormous birds that they can be around a fifth bigger than the White-tailed Eagles that nest in Scotland and boast wingspans that can be – at reportedly up to nine and a half feet – considerably broader. Although they are said to be the most aggressive and powerful African vultures, and can tear up a meal in a way that is helpful to weaker species, they will often stand on the periphery, waiting for smaller birds to have their fill before devouring the tougher parts of an animal that are left over. Competition for food can be brutal in the wild but vultures enjoy an obvious advantage over hyenas and other scavengers in that they can spot a dead or dying animal from greater distances. The Lappet-faced Vulture will either identify a carcass itself or follow other vultures to a kill. I photographed one of these enormous birds at the feeding frenzy, its huge brown wings steered by a pale blue, white and deep pink face, and fronted by a darkly magnificent hooked beak that had no doubt torn its way through many a tendon.

While vultures may understandably be seen as angels of death, they do play an important role within their habitats. By devouring the decaying animals that litter a landscape, they help prevent the spread of disease. Not only that, but if you're lucky enough to frame with your camera a vulture sitting high in a tree against the setting sun, it can provide jaw-dropping images of evening in the bush. With the help of Charles's keen eye and his years of experience, I was able to take some of the most beautiful shots of our entire safari by photographing these grotesque birds silhouetted against glowing balls of yellow and orange. And the fact I couldn't distinguish between the Lappet-Faced, White-backed, Ruppell's, Hooded and White-headed Vultures in distant silhouette, doesn't detract from the strength of the images!

Vulture,
Masai Mara, Kenya

SECRETARY BIRD (112-152cm)

How better to close this book than with one of the strangest birds on earth. The Secretary Bird is so named, it's thought, because its crest of quill-like feathers resembles the pens tucked into the wigs of 18th century clerks. It looks like a cross between a stork and a bird of prey and while it nests and roosts in the tops of acacia trees, unusually for a raptor it hunts on the ground. Its long, comical legs are used to stalk quarry through the grasses of the African savannah, and then sometimes also to stomp on and stun or kill it. The Secretary Bird also makes use of its big, strong feet to stamp the ground in a bid to flush a meal from its hiding place. Victims can include mongoose, hares, venomous snakes and lizards and smaller prey is swallowed whole. Although these surprising looking raptors are good fliers, they have to run some distance before being able to take off.

The red-pink, orange and yellow skin on the faces of Secretary Birds offer a colourful contrast to the mix of greys, white and black of the body and wing feathers. I photographed one of these remarkable specimens striding across the Mara in the rain, its coat shaggy in the wet, but I had greater luck when our guide, Charles, spotted one preening itself on top of an acacia tree. A more different bird to the Coal Tits I have watched feed and sing in Britain, you would struggle to find. And that is one of the joys of birdwatching and bird photography: the mind-bending variety of the birds that make up the avian communities with which we are so lucky to share our world.

above and opposite: Secretary Bird, Masai Mara, Kenya

INDEX

BIBLIOGRAPHY

Allaboutbirds.org
Animalcorner.co.uk
Animalfactguide.com
Animals.mom.me
Audubon.org
Barnowltrust.org
Bbc.co.uk
Bbog.co.uk
Beautyofbirds.com
Birding.krugerpark.co.za
Birdingmalta.com
Britishbirdlovers.co.uk
Britishbirdofpreycentre.co.uk
Bto.org
Cam.ac.uk

Chesterzoo.com
Dailymail.co.uk
Discoverwildlife.com
Ducksters.com
Globalanimal.org
Gmwildlife.org
Guardian.com
Gwct.org.uk
Habitas.org.uk
Hbw.com
Howstuffworks.com
Independent.co.uk
Livescience.com
Livingwithbirds.com
Nationalgeographic.com

Oceanwide-expeditions.com
Oiseaux-birds.com
Pressandjournal.co.uk
Rspb.org.uk
Seaturtles.com
Seaworld.org
Telegraph.co.uk
Thegreatcraneproject.org
Themysteriousworld.com
Thetravelalmanac.com
Wikipedia.org
Wildlifetrusts.org
Wildscreen.com
Woodlandtrust.org

For more details on the websites used to research this book please visit: ***http://papadakis.net/how-to-see-birds-bibliography***

ACKNOWLEDGEMENTS

I would like first to thank my publisher and editor, Alexandra Papadakis. She believed in this book and in my passion for telling its story through photographs and words. Without her commitment to ambitious projects such as this, *How To See Birds* might never have happened. Together with her team - Aldo Sampieri and Megan Prudden - she has helped me to realise a dream. I'd also like to put on record my gratitude to my parents, Frances and Nick, who have always believed in me, supported me and encouraged me to fulfil my potential in whatever it is that I set my mind to. Both have championed my photography and love of nature. I am thankful, too, to my uncle and godfather, David Howarth, who took me to see my first Golden Eagle and Ospreys in Scotland when I was just eight years old: he helped instil in me my love of birdwatching. It is important also to send thanks to all those who work so hard in this country to protect birds from the many threats they face and who encourage the rest of us to enjoy them responsibly. Special appreciation goes to Martin Harper, the Global Conservation Director of the RSPB, for his generous introduction. Our neighbour in Wales, Mike Haigh, does important bird-related work, has helped introduce me to new species and was kind enough to check through my writing - I am in his debt. Finally, and most of all, I'd like to thank my wife, Lily Walters, for celebrating who I am and for taking pleasure in the pleasure I take in watching and photographing birds.

Matthew Stadlen is a radio and television presenter. He began presenting on LBC in October 2016 and has achieved large national audiences for his weekend shows. He interviews famous names on stage at venues around the country and presents a podcast series for *How To Academy*.

He presented, produced and co-devised the hugely successful *Five Minutes With* interview strand as well as 29 half hour *On The Road With* documentaries – both for the BBC, where he was also a programme editor on BBC One's *This Week* after starting out on *Newsnight*.

Matthew made national and international headlines with his articles for *The Telegraph* and wrote *The Matthew Stadlen Interview* in the paper. He has written for *The Sunday Times* and *Radio Times*, *The Independent* and *The Spectator*, he has appeared frequently on *Sky News* and is the co-author of *The Politics Companion*, published in 2004.

Cambridge educated, Matthew was born and raised in Notting Hill where he still lives but he gets out to the country whenever he can to pursue his twin passions of photography and birdwatching. He has photographed over 200 species and seen around 900. Find him on Twitter and Instagram @matthewstadlen.